Tips & Trips of Parenting a New Age Kid

Sandra K. Jones-Keller

Illustrations by Thomas Keller

Halo
PUBLISHING
INTERNATIONAL

Also by Sandra K. Jones-Keller

Intuitive Communication With Your Baby's Soul

21 Lessons To Empower The New Age Kid

How I Beat Fibroid Tumors For A Successful Pregnancy Over 40

For information about this book or other services,
contact the author at SandraJonesKeller.com.

ISBN: 978-1-63765-133-9
LCCN: 2021921299

Halo Publishing International, LLC
8000 W Interstate 10, Suite 600
San Antonio, Texas 78230
www.halopublishing.com

Printed and bound in the United States of America

For all the moms, dads, grandparents,
and caregivers doing your best to raise
a happy and healthy kid.

CONTENTS

ACKNOWLEDGMENTS

his book would not be possible without the contributions of my amazing family—my husband, Thomas, and daughter, Mecca. Thank you, Thomas, for being my co-pilot on this journey of life and parenthood. For always encouraging me to *go for it*, no matter what the *it*, is. Mecca, being your mom has expanded me in ways I didn't know were possible. Thank you for choosing me to love and guide you through this lifetime.

I've had so much support and encouragement along the way to completing this book. Thank you to Rhonda Sabir for reviewing each and every story with me, and to JC Bronsted for your concise and detailed notes. A heartfelt shou-tout goes to my Wednesday night writer's group, led by Kristine Gill, for your diligence, patience, and instrumental feedback as this book unfolded; and to my teachers Jim Robison and Karla Araujo, and classmates at the Renaissance Academy for providing indispensable suggestions and inspiration. And thank you to Alison Blanco for your keen eye and sincere assistance.

INTRODUCTION

hat you're about to read is not a "How To" parenting book. I'm not going to teach you how to discipline your children or how to make them do what you want when you want. I'm going to share my family's particular journey of raising a New Age Kid through a series of personal and heartfelt essays involving our daughter, Mecca.

My husband and I are not experts in child development. We're parents just like you trying to do the best for our kid. Each moment is new, each stage an adventure. We've never raised a daughter before so we're working it out moment to moment. But, what we do have is an arsenal of tools that we use to support our relationship and our parenting style that I'll share with you. Easy techniques that don't take long to learn, however, they do require perseverance and commitment on your part.

Why not just use traditional discipline, fear or coercion?

Because getting my daughter to modify her behavior to fit my needs is not the same as healing an issue.

Once I/we can pinpoint a problem, we can actually heal it so that we ALL have harmony as opposed to temporary fixes in behavioral concerns. What's the benefit to you? Peace, fewer power struggles, more laughter, less anxiety, and a balanced, grounded child!

Years ago, I attended a spiritual relationship retreat with my then-boyfriend, now-husband Thomas. I was armed with my list of issues I wanted to complain about to our teacher. Boy, was it long! I couldn't wait to hash out all of my grievances concerning Thomas and the way he did things in front of someone who would sympathize with my plight. I was eager to hear how right I was from the other women in the group.

Imagine my disappointment when the first thing out of our teacher's mouth was, "You are only in a relationship with yourself." Say, what?

What about my list? I have some really good stuff on here, I wanted to ask, but didn't.

"Everyone is a mirror of yourself," she explained. "If you're seeing or experiencing something in your life that you don't like, look within to see where you're doing it, or who you're being." I felt like she looked directly at me when she said this. I slouched in my seat to be less exposed.

I was tempted to get up and leave. My ego didn't like what I was hearing. This wasn't my plan at all. But, since we had traveled from Los Angeles to North Carolina to get there, it wasn't easy to just take off. Besides, I had nowhere to go and nothing else to do. If I walked out of the retreat, I'd be spending the next couple of days in a room by myself because I could tell Thomas was going to stay.

I took a deep breath and tried to surrender to the experience. *Maybe, just maybe this won't be awful*, I hoped. I had attended other meetings that had been enlightening and uplifting. Now, I would settle for satisfactory since my initial hopes had been squashed.

Let's just say I walked away profoundly changed. I learned tools and techniques that not only improved my relationship with Thomas, but became the primary parenting practices we use with our daughter.

You see, too often, we as parents view our children's attitudes and behaviors as separate from ourselves. As something outside of us that needs to be controlled or corrected if we consider it a problem—just like I did with Thomas before attending the relationship retreat. Stay with me here: but if/since "Everyone is a mirror of myself," then my daughter is as well. As our teacher said, "If I'm seeing it, I'm being it." Well, if I'm seeing Mecca do something that disturbs me, then after I get over my annoyance or irritation, I look within to see where I'm doing that thing. For example, I can ask her a question and she'll give me a one-word answer or vague response.

"How was co-op today?"

"Fine."

"What did you do?"

"Science and art."

"What did you do in science?"

"An experiment."

You get the picture. But if I'm honest, I do the exact same thing if I don't feel like talking at that moment or at all. Do you see where I'm going with this? How many parents have you heard talk about their uncontrollable anxiety only to be befuddled later that their child suffers from stress and anxiousness?

Let's keep going. Okay, so I see the behavior that disturbs me and I've identified where I do the same thing. What's next? I try to knock it off. When/if I catch myself withholding my answers, I share more. I contribute to the conversation rather than making it as difficult as pulling teeth to talk to me.

I also practice an ancient Hawaiian forgiveness technique developed by Dr. Hew Len, co-author of *Zero Limits,* called ho'oponopono. By repeating these four phrases to myself silently or out loud: "I'm Sorry", "Please Forgive Me", "I Love You", "Thank You", over and over, I'm giving forth (forgiving) the part of me that withholds or does that thing that someone is showing me. Remember, I said the tools are easy to learn but require commitment and perseverance on your part. There are times when I don't want to acknowledge the mirror in front of me or I really don't like seeing how my actions caused a certain outcome like in my essay *He Got Two Presents, I Got Nada* (page 110). But, by sticking with mirroring and forgiveness work, situations transformed and miracles occurred in ways I couldn't have imagined. You'll understand more as you dive deeper into this book.

As I said, the relationship retreat was life changing—it took the onus off of Thomas to change and turned it back on me to be more introspective. That's not to say we don't ever point fingers of blame at each other, or even at our daughter, but ultimately, we come back to mirroring and forgiveness work for healing and resolutions of family issues and concerns.

You may find this surprising, but other tools in our parenting arsenal include using Universal Laws to bring awareness and understanding to matters. The Law of Mentalism states we live in a mental Universe, and that everything begins with a thought; the Golden Rule tells us to do unto others as you would have them do unto you. In other words, if you don't want to be stolen from, don't steal. If you don't want to be lied to, don't lie. If you don't want to be cheated, don't cheat. Basically, we talk to Mecca about her agency in creating her life; how her thoughts, actions and behaviors draw to her positive and negative experiences. This gives her the capacity to check-in with herself and decide if she likes the way things are going, and if not, she has the tools to change them IF she chooses to use them.

> **As parents, we cannot protect our children from the consequences of Universal Laws. These Laws are always in operation and govern life whether we're aware of them or believe in them or not.**

My husband and I noticed that many of the kids born today are unlike those from previous generations. These old souls are far more attuned to their connection to other people and the Universe. As my daughter puts it, "I know I'm part of something bigger." With this in mind, we feel many parenting techniques from the past are outdated. Just 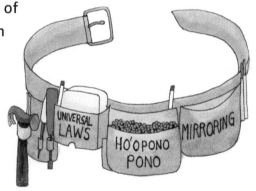 doing something because our ancestors did it that way doesn't make sense to us in this day and age. The times are different and the kids are different. So, what's a parent to do?

Our answer was to lean into our spiritual teachings: incorporate the same methods that saved our relationship into our parenting style. Treat Mecca like the intelligent, conscious being that we know she is. Create a partnership with her for her upbringing, not a dictatorship. Provide a loving and supportive environment and seek out opportunities that excite and interest her. Stay away from

"Because I said so!" and replace with "Because I asked you to." Make requests, not demands.

When I was pregnant, I had developed intuitive two-way communication with Mecca. I talked to my unborn daughter and she answered back. Our telepathic (an internal voice I heard in my head) conversations helped me have a successful full term high-risk pregnancy. She had a very clear, certain and wise voice. We developed a partnership before her birth which has continued to this day. I talk more about my experience and process in my essay *How Does Intuitive Communication Help You Raise a New Age Kid?* (page 24), in the Before Birth section of this book.

Some of the stories in this book are sweet, some are humorous, and some may be difficult for you to believe, like Mecca healing a lump on her neck in *That Cyst Isn't Going Away* (page 128). Sometimes Thomas and I seem like the smartest parents in the world, and sometimes you may think, *What the heck are they doing?* like in my piece *I Accused Her of Being Unprepared* (page 113). No matter the tone, each story has a nugget that I hope will give you a new perspective on raising these amazing old souls that have come into our lives to shift paradigms and break down long-standing structures that don't work.

Ultimately, I like to think of parenting as an evolutionary process. We don't know what we don't know and are constantly making adjustments and corrections as situations arise. We're doing our best to raise a conscious, compassionate child who will be a magnificent contribution to humanity—and like most parents, we're not perfect. But our daughter definitely knows she is loved and supported on her journey throughout this lifetime.

HOW TO USE THIS BOOK

s you peruse this book, take your time. Let the material sink in. Place your-self inside the stories and ask, "What would I do in that situation?" Some of the stories even have Ice Breaker questions at the end. Digest them solely, and discuss together as a family. Open up the dialogue even more by getting your child's viewpoint. You may be surprised by what they think.

Remember, this is not a child-rearing book. I'm not telling you how to raise your children or what you should or shouldn't do—I'm simply sharing my family's personal experiences and journey over the years. Like in my essay, *A Bedtime Alarm?* (page 79), I talk about my struggles of getting Mecca to bed at an early hour and how letting her self-regulate her bedtime ended our nightly battles. And in *Don't Wake Me Up to Eat* (page 36), we quickly learned to trust our newborn's internal clock which regulated her eating schedule perfectly and made her a much happier baby. Refer to the essays time and again, and maybe even get a head start on tackling future matters as your child grows older.

The book is divided into five sections by age range, including Before Birth stories that set the foundation for our commitment and philosophy as parents. Also, each section begins with a homeschool story that further illustrates our values. You can skip around or read it in order: each essay is a self-contained story with its own tidbit of information and doesn't rely on other essays to be understandable and usable.

Most importantly, have fun reading! The stories can be enjoyed by new parents, seasoned mothers and fathers, aunts and uncles, caregivers, empty nesters, or even grandparents; the book encompasses universal themes to be enjoyed by any age or stage or life. In the end, you can gain new insights and perspectives and have your very own 'aha' moments over and over even if you don't agree with our philosophy or choices.

* * *

Note to Readers:

The author of this book does not give out medical advice or prescribe the use of any technique as a form of treatment for physical or medical problems. The intent of the author is only to offer personal examples of alternatives used to foster awareness to help you in your quest of raising a New Age kid. In the event you use any of the information in this book for yourself or your child, which is your constitutional right, the author and the publisher assume no responsibility for your actions.

BEFORE BIRTH

HOW WE DECIDED TO HOMESCHOOL

t was strange that Thomas and I decided to homeschool our child before I was pregnant and before we had even talked about having a baby. Our relationship was still fairly new and we were having one of many *getting to know you conversations*.

We sat cross-legged on top of the covers on the bed, backs against the headboard, periodically glancing out the sun-drenched window in my townhouse as we asked each other a variety of questions about growing up, family life, likes and dislikes. Despite Thomas being white and me being black, and raised in different parts of the U.S.—him in a small country town in western Kentucky, me in the suburbs near Disneyland in Southern California—we had similar backgrounds. Both of us came from two parent households with dads that worked, moms who stayed home and raised kids during our primary years, and a continuous, arduous search for God and meaning in our lives. Our discussion flowed easily and jumped from subject to subject like a bee pollinating rich, vibrant flowers. Homeschooling sort of came up out of the blue.

I had read that millions of families in the U.S. and around the world home-school their children for a variety of reasons. Some include dissatisfaction with academic instruction at schools and safety and security concerns at these establishments, religious or moral grounds, fear of bullying or peer pressure, and the ability to choose what and how their kids learn.

Our reasons were closest to the latter—we wanted to leave space for our child to hear their own inner wisdom and direction, which can get lost or go silent when excessive facts and figures take up brain space. If we homeschooled, we could control what, and how our child learned; we wouldn't bombard them with information for information's sake, and they would be encouraged to follow their heart and interests.

We had witnessed and experienced the frustration of traditional education stuffing us with material that we never used or was irrelevant to our lives. We had spent countless hours memorizing data just to pass a test. We desired something different for our offspring, and committed to a homeschool program should we ever have a child together.

Prior to meeting Thomas in *A Course In Miracles* (*ACIM*) study group in Los Angeles, I had been on my own spiritual quest for over 15 years and had been an energy healer for 10. I traveled to sacred sites in Mexico, Guatemala, Costa Rica, and Peru, mostly alone, occasionally with friends, to connect with the healing energy of the planet. I sat on primeval ruins contemplating life and my purpose in it. I was in my first year of Practitioner training (I didn't complete the entire two-year program due to a high-risk pregnancy) to be a Religious Science Spiritual Counselor through Agape International Spiritual Center, and had dreamed of sharing this life with my next partner. My former husband had not been interested in *anything* metaphysical.

Thomas was a self-described wandering loner and truth seeker. In fact, he had already planned to move to Asheville, North Carolina before we officially started dating, and I lived in Los Angeles, so the first six months of our relationship was long distance. He traveled the globe studying ancient cultures and had completed many transformational programs throughout the years. He also attended Agape and was deeply immersed in an Egyptian Mystery School with the same group that had studied *ACIM*. He was in his late 40's, never married, no children, and ready to find his life partner. Like me, he wanted to share his passion and interest in the mystical with his mate.

Once during a conversation about travelling, Thomas reminisced about his trip to the ancient Mayan ruins in the jungles of Palenque, Mexico.

"I'll go there with you," I blurted out.

"Really?" His voice raised in disbelief.

"Oh yeah. I love travelling through Mexico and Central America. I feel most at home there. I'm way more relaxed and peaceful in that region of the world."

A shocked smile crossed his face. "I didn't think I'd find someone who'd want to travel to Palenque with me."

I grinned too—I had finally found a companion to share my adventures with as well.

＊ ＊ ＊

Studying *ACIM* and Religious Science gave Thomas and I similar principles and teachings about the importance of children maintaining their awareness and connection to their divine selves (spirit, true-self, authentic-self, higher-self, God-self, as opposed to the personality or ego). We learned that if that connection is not actively fostered it can go to sleep around seven years old. I had lost my awareness as a child and took two decades to reestablish it; my husband slowly found his way over 40 years. Self-awareness was to be a critical part of our curriculum.

A few short weeks after our conversation, I became pregnant, and our seemingly premature discussion about homeschooling made sense. Thinking back, I sometimes wonder if our daughter planted those seeds in our consciousness. I don't remember if I had ever considered homeschooling before, but, in that moment, I was absolutely sure it was the thing I wanted most to do.

HOW DOES INTUITIVE COMMUNICATION HELP YOU RAISE YOUR NEW AGE KID?

hroughout the years, I've been asked a variety of questions based on the relationship I created with my daughter before she was born.

Question: "How does having pre-birth communication actually help you raise your kid?"

Answer: "In a myriad of ways."

Question: "Is your daughter some kind of spiritual guru?"

Answer: "No."

Question: "Does she like to meditate and do all sorts of woo-woo stuff?"

Answer: "Not at all."

Question: "Well, what's the point then?"

Answer: "Great question."

In my book *Intuitive Communication With Your Baby's Soul*, I recount the journey of my high-risk pregnancy, which led to a surprising and unexpected partnership with my unborn little one:

At 41 years old, I became pregnant with my daughter Mecca. Before I even went to the doctor, I knew something was off. I was only a few days late with my cycle, but I looked like I was 3-4 months pregnant. Turns out I had a couple of large fibroid tumors, one of which was at the base of my uterus. The doctor's prognosis for me was pretty dire: I'd be bedridden for most of my pregnancy, Mecca would be born 3 months premature, and I would have a C-section.

I did what I always do when confronted with a challenge or fear. I got busier and deeper into my spiritual practices. I began meditating more. I spent time in quiet contemplation and reflection. I did spiritual mind treatments (affirmative prayer) with a practitioner. I connected with nature, read my spiritual books, wrote out positive affirmations, and most of all, I listened deeply and intently to my intuition.

What ensued over the next 8 ½ months was a partnership between me and my unborn daughter to have a healthy and successful pregnancy. I did have a C-section, but I carried her full term. I was never bedridden. As a matter of fact, I worked part-time up until the weekend before she was born. And Mecca came home at the end of my hospital stay. How did I beat my prognosis? I developed intuitive two-way communication with my baby. I talked to my unborn daughter and she answered back! Yes, she answered back!

I was about three months pregnant the first time Mecca talked back to me. Thomas and I were at a spiritual conference in Las Vegas. We were scheduled to return to Los Angeles on Monday. What Thomas hadn't told me was that he had checked us out of our room on Sunday and we were going to spend the last night with his friend (to save some money.) Well, I was pregnant and uncomfortable and very annoyed. I didn't want to share a room with someone else, so I told him I would catch a ride back to Los Angeles. He totally surprised me by asking, "Did you ask Mecca what she wants to do?"

My first thought was, *Why do I need to ask her? It's my body, I get to decide.* But I thought I would humor him. I went into meditation, quieted my mind and asked Mecca, "Do you want to go home with me or stay in Vegas with Daddy?" Before I barely finished the question, I heard a voice in my mind say, "I want to stay here with Daddy." Now this was not the answer I wanted! I had my own agenda, I wanted to go home and thought for sure that she would want to go with me. Not to be deterred, I asked her again—the same answer. I knew this was her voice because the answer wasn't what I wanted to hear. I went back to Thomas and begrudgingly said, "We're staying."

After my first two-way telepathic (an internal voice I heard in my head) conversation with Mecca in Las Vegas, she and I had access to a deeper level of communication. Before this, I had been simply talking to her, rubbing my belly and loving her silently. Now I knew she could and would answer back!

I began to rely on her feedback and wisdom to support me during my pregnancy. I was quite emotional and often scared after several of my doctor's appointments. My doctor would say with complete confidence things like, "Mecca will be born early because your uterus can only stretch so far and you are pretty close to that maximum." Or, "There's a chance your fibroids might interfere with the growth of your baby." At one point they couldn't find her heartbeat after extensive searching. But, she had carved a space for herself in between my fibroids and was hanging out there comfortably.

Almost daily I would ask Mecca how she was doing. Her answer was always the same, "I'm fine mom, take care of yourself." I could feel her strong, loving, confident energy ushering me along the way. Because I knew she was fine, I had the strength and determination to focus on myself, doing what I needed to do to carry her safely to full-term.

What the doctors didn't know that I knew was that there was a higher power than the medical profession that I was calling on throughout my pregnancy and delivery. I call it God, some may call it Spirit, Holy Spirit, Allah, Christ, angels; you may call it whatever is comfortable for you. This Universal Power completely supported and guided me on this journey. My doctors and nurses had based their predictions on what they had seen in the past. Had I bought into the medical professional's experiences, then my original prognosis probably would have occurred. Fortunately, I had my spiritual toolbox to pull from, which assisted me in creating a different reality than the predictions I had received.

After Mecca was born, I would check in with her telepathically to see if she had woken up if I was downstairs and she was upstairs, or ask her how she was feeling if she didn't look like her normal self. I still check in with her telepathically even after all these years. I do this by getting quiet, closing my eyes, and focusing on reaching out to her higher self. I like to call it Mother's intuition stepped up!

※ ※ ※

Now what does this have to do with raising a kid you may wonder? For me, everything!

First and foremost, I know and understand my daughter is a spiritual being. I know that the life she's living is not just about this physical world—she has a purpose that's all her own and I am here to guide her—to be a partner and way-shower as she learns to navigate Earth. She's not my possession and she wasn't born because I wanted to be a mother or anything like that. It's not my job to plan out her life, but to provide exposure to the world (we like to travel, she's tried several sports and we love various forms of entertainment, especially live theater). Most importantly, it's our responsibility to show her continually that she's deeply loved and unconditionally accepted.

So, when I get caught up in the day-to-day stuff, and start being pushy or overbearing, I have to remind myself that Mecca is self-aware, motivated, and is an intelligent being that has her own intuitive connection to a higher power. Some days I do a much better job at this than others, but my overall intention dictates how I communicate and interact with my daughter ongoingly.

Occasionally though, I wonder if my kid missed out on some of the childhood fantasies I enjoyed growing up like believing in Santa Claus and the Tooth Fairy. Since we've always viewed Mecca as an old soul, it didn't make sense to us to teach her about fictional characters that would have to be unexplained later. It felt like we would be betraying her trust in us by telling her things we knew weren't true. Alas, I have no cute pictures of her grinning awkwardly while sitting on Santa's lap at the mall and she always knew that we put the money under her pillow for lost teeth.

Even when she was an infant, I'd cringe at people who wanted to baby-talk to her. I imagined her active brain thinking something like, *Just because I'm adorable and cuddly and in this baby's body doesn't mean I'm unaware.* Thomas and I talked to her like we talked to each other because we knew she understood us on a deeper level. I would even ask her questions like, "Do you like this?" while feeding her homemade organic baby food or "Would you like to go out today?" She couldn't answer me verbally, therefore I would listen internally for her response the same way I did while she was still in my belly.

Ultimately, being a mom is a balancing act of living in the physical world and remembering my daughter's true essence. Like all parents we want to keep our child safe and happy, and that means different things at different times. I will often sit quietly and check in with my intuition when my daughter is invited to go somewhere or wants to try something new. If the energy doesn't feel peaceful and harmonious, the answer will be no, even if on the surface the activity makes sense. For example, Mecca was invited to go ice skating with family friends one Sunday night. The energy felt off to me so I declined the invitation. Turns out they got to the rink and it was closed for a special event. Listening to my intuition saved my daughter from a disappointing outing that night.

As we continue to navigate life and parenthood, as well as grow and develop, I lean on the earliest communication with my child to keep me sane in this hectic world. This reminds me that she is guided and protected by a higher source, and I trust that together we can get through anything, just like we did with my high-risk pregnancy.

ICE BREAKERS:

Parents: Do you have any examples/experiences of using intuition in your parenting?

How Does Intuitive Communication Help You Raise Your New Age Kid?

Sandra, "I still tune in. As a matter of fact just the other day you and I were out and I said I'm going home because it's raining and I know she doesn't like the rain, and no sooner than I was driving home, five minutes later she called me and asked me when I was coming home because intuitively I felt it."

Link: https://youtu.be/qST7WANT3H0

0-3 YEARS

HOMESCHOOLING 101—STORYTIME

ust because Thomas and I had committed to homeschooling our daughter before she was born, didn't mean we knew how. It was an internal impulse that guided us along the way. We treated everything we did like it was an opportunity for growth and learning. We'd take time to explain things even when Mecca couldn't verbally answer back, and we'd answer questions with questions as she grew older, getting her to think and reason even as a toddler. Little did we know that nightly storytime would be an integral jumping off point for my daughter's education.

I started reading out loud to my newborn almost as soon as we arrived home from the hospital. Although I was recovering from my stressful C-section, I enjoyed cradling her in my arms and escaping into the worlds of Dr. Seuss and Biscuit before putting her to bed. Thomas would lift Mecca from her crib in our bedroom and hand her gently to me while I leaned upright against the headboard. I had read about the positive effects of storytelling from a clinical perspective, but I was surprised by the pleasure I received bonding with my little one night after night over these tall tales. I don't remember my parents reading to me as a youngster and I so appreciated this experience with my child.

For the first 6 years of her life, Mecca and I did storytime almost every night before she went to bed. I even packed a couple of her favorite books to take with us on trips like *Angelina Ballerina* by Helen Craig or *The Tooth Book* by Dr. Seuss. We curled up reading in hotel rooms and vacation rentals. It was our personal ritual as Thomas didn't really enjoy it—he, instead, painted and did other creative activities with her. We started with bright and colorful picture books that had few words like *D Is For Dolphin* by Cami Berg and *The Little Engine That Could* by Watty Piper Read. My daughter listened attentively as I described the scene on the page, at first gurgling with glee, then pointing and poking at the characters with her pudgy fingers as she developed more dexterity. We enjoyed all sorts of fun stories from classic fairy tales to cultural parables. We read *Reading: Picture This!* by Scott Foresman night after night. There were so many captivating and diverse tales in this one book that she was introduced to words and images from around the globe, thus becoming a citizen of the world early on. Another favorite was *I Like Myself!* by Karen Beaumont which encouraged my daughter to like and accept everything about herself.

Storytime grew as Mecca grew. Not only did we read together, we also did search and find books. She learned to see patterns and identify objects and slowly began recognizing and sounding out words. Around three years old she memorized *Biscuit* by Alyssa Satin Capucilli and would verbalize the story while turning the pages, making it look like she was actually reading. I adored watching her pretend to read and listened intently as she told the story verbatim. When she was done, I'd squeeze and kiss her whilst acknowledging her wonderful skills. She'd smile and poke her chest out with pride, then we'd giggle and find another book to complete our evening.

In addition to reading at home, we went to a local bookstore twice a week for their group storytime events. Most of the kids sat on the floor while the parents milled around in the back alternating between listening to the stories and chatting with each other. Mecca met her first set of friends at these gatherings. The facilitator chose lively, interesting books which she read with verve and enthusiasm that further fostered my daughter's love of books and reading. We still remember the tune the group leader sang while reading *I Ain't Gonna Paint No More!* by Karen Beaumont.

Our routine shifted as Mecca stayed up later and later. In the beginning, I tucked her in after finishing our stories. Around 4 years old, when her bedtime shifted to 1:00 a.m. (refer to *A Bedtime Alarm* essay), I'd read to her, then kiss her goodnight instead of tucking her in. She would then color or play with her toys until she went to bed.

Eventually, around 6 years old, our nightly storytime came to an end. By this time Mecca was reading simple books and our ritual naturally fizzled out. It began feeling forced—we would stop whatever else we were doing, read a quick story, then go back to our respective activities. We ultimately agreed that we were complete with this phase of our lives and I felt that I had given it my all.

It's funny how things circle back. Fast forward a few years, Mecca and I started listening to audiobooks in the car, though it was sometimes difficult to find one we agreed on:

"That's not interesting." Mecca.

"I don't like the main character." Me.

"It's too slow." Mecca.

"I can't stand the narrator." Both of us.

"That story has no relevance to my life." Me.

And so on. We searched and searched until we found an audiobook we both liked, then sat back and enjoyed the tale just like we did during our nightly storytimes years ago.

* * *

In hindsight, I see how reading aloud to my daughter laid a foundation for her strong language skills and expanded her vocabulary exponentially by subtly teaching her the rules of grammar and phonics while we snuggled together each night with our books. And reading continues to play a key role not only in her education but her recreation time as well. She loves various types of books, but manga, fantasy, and supernatural stories are her favorites. Ultimately, I feel Mecca's early exposure to words and worlds beyond our four walls supported her in becoming an impressive storyteller that writes creative, imaginative and entertaining short tales and contributed to her confidence in communicating and learning overall.

DON'T WAKE ME UP TO EAT

ave you ever been chewed out by a newborn? It's actually quite jarring to say the least. "Waah, waah, waah," in high pitched screams followed by unsteady breathing, hiccupping, and more waahs.

I had had a planned C-section and was exhausted and overwhelmed. My delivery and post-surgery recovery took longer than most because of my fruit sized fibroid tumors, so I was especially thankful that our hospital had beautiful pregnancy suites where we could all stay together in the room after Mecca's birth. Thomas had a comfy sofa to sleep on underneath the window and my daughter's crib was near my bed in the middle of the room.

As first-time parents, Thomas and I felt the doctors and nurses in the hospital knew way more than we did about caring for our daughter. So, when the staff told us we needed to feed our daughter every couple of hours, it sounded reasonable to us at first, except:

"Well, what if she's sleeping?" Thomas asked the nurse instructing us.

"Then you wake her up." I thought I heard her say 'duh', but I wasn't sure.

"Hmm. Won't she just wake up if she's hungry?" I asked.

"Babies need to build their strength so it's important they eat every two to three hours," the nurse explained, speaking slowly.

"But what if she's not hungry?" Thomas asked.

"Babies need to eat regularly," she said with finality.

"Okay," we agreed, not wanting to be difficult because we felt that we really did need her help and advice.

In the middle of the first night, Thomas gently woke Mecca up for her feeding and brought her to me in the bed. Let's just say she wasn't happy. She had been sleeping peacefully—now she screamed so loudly they probably heard her across the courtyard.

If I could interpret Mecca's words, I think she said, "Are you kidding me? Don't you think I'm smart enough to eat when I'm hungry? You messed up my dream. When I'm hungry, I will let you know. In the meantime, if I'm asleep, Don't. Wake. Me. Up! Now I'm just cranky."

I laid her on my chest to soothe her. She continued to wail. I tried placing my nipple in her mouth, but she wouldn't take it. Finally, Thomas rocked her back to sleep and put her in her crib.

"What the hell?" I said after it had quieted down.

"We're not doing that again."

"What do we tell the nurses when they ask if we fed her?"

"Tell them what happened," Thomas said.

"This is crazy. I communicated with Mecca all through my pregnancy and she was always very clear about what she needed."

Thomas just hunched his shoulders and sighed.

"How are you doing this morning?" the nurse asked when she came to check on me and my little one.

"Okay," I said.

"When was the last time the baby ate?" she asked, standing next to my bed, back straight, eyes focused and looking very authoritative.

I glanced at Thomas for support. "Sometime last night."

"You're supposed to feed her every couple of hours," the nurse reminded me.

"Well, we woke her up and she screamed her head off. She wasn't hungry and didn't even eat," Thomas explained.

"She needs to eat. It's okay if she cries but you need to get her to eat," the nurse explained again.

"It just seems to me that she'll eat when she's ready. She was really upset that we woke her up," I said.

Thomas shook his head at me before I could continue with my brilliant reasoning.

"Okay," he said to the nurse.

"Good," she said and left.

Annoyed he'd cut me off, I asked, "Why'd you do that?"

"Because the hospital has a policy about feeding babies and we're not going to change their minds."

"I'm not waking her up again. That was a nightmare."

"Neither am I," Thomas said in a whisper. "We'll be vague when they ask us about it."

"Oh, okay," I agreed. We were like teenagers plotting to get out of trouble.

For the next couple of days, we became very elusive about Mecca's eating schedule.

"Has the baby eaten recently?"

"Yes."

"When was the last time the baby ate?"

"Hmm, not too long ago. Thomas, do you remember when Mecca ate?"

"Yeah, seems like she just ate," he'd say.

When Mecca was hungry, she ate a great deal then drifted back to sleep, peacefully!

Since there were a few different nurses checking in on us, we kept up the charade without too much difficulty. Mecca was healthy and thriving, as a result, there was no need for the staff to be concerned.

We followed the same eating protocol after we arrived home: I breastfed my newborn as often as she wanted for as long as she wanted, however, we never woke her up to eat. Little did we know that learning to trust our parenting instincts and our daughter's cues at the hospital was the first step to letting Mecca self-regulate many things in her life.

AND I REALLY LIKED THOSE SHOES

don't remember exactly how it all started, but one day, Mecca threw a toy at me while I was driving. I yelped in shock, she laughed, and a nasty pattern was set in motion.

When you're 3 years old, annoying a parent is very funny.

Fortunately, she didn't do this every day, although her timing was impeccable. It would happen when I was maneuvering through heavy traffic or waiting to make a left turn from a busy intersection.

I tried reasoning with her. "Mecca, please don't throw things at Mommy while I'm driving. It's dangerous and distracting. I need to pay attention and getting

smacked in the head or having your toy slam into the windshield startles Mommy and I could hit someone. Do you understand?"

A slight nod yes with an underlying sly smile was her response.

I tried getting mad. "Stop throwing things at me!"

Low grade giggles.

I tried being wounded. "Mecca, it really hurts Mommy's feelings when you fling your toys at me. Please don't do that."

Blank stare.

Then, one day as I changed lanes on the bustling highway with big rigs pushing in on both sides, my daughter hurled a shoe at me. The black leather ballet slipper crashed into the windshield, ricocheted off the steering wheel, and struck me in the face. My startled shriek brought roaring chuckles from the backseat.

I grabbed the ballet slipper and was about to toss it to her when I had an epiphany that I thought might end this madness: instead of returning her shoe like I had done many times before, I rolled down the passenger window, pointed to the window to make sure she saw exactly what I was doing, and heaved her new flat out onto the side of the road, all while speeding down the interstate.

Her giggles instantly turned into screams. "No, No, NO!" She squealed as we drove farther and farther away from her discarded footwear.

"I'm sorry honey, but I had to do it."

"My shoe, my shoe!" she screeched through streams of tears.

"Yeah, I know. And I just bought you those shoes last week. I really liked those ballet slippers too," I said in my calmest voice.

I finally turned up the radio to drown out her sobbing—she whimpered the whole drive home.

After she calmed down, we had a brief chat about the incident.

"Honey, I'm so sorry I threw your shoe out the window, but I felt like I had to do something drastic to get your attention."

"My new shoe," she pouted.

"Yep, I know. Make you a deal—you don't throw things at me while I'm driving, and I won't throw your stuff out the window?"

"Okay," she agreed. No sly smirks, or giggles or blank stares. Just an authentic okay. And she really meant it that time—she never flung an object at me again while I sat behind the wheel of my car.

ICE BREAKERS:

Parents: What's the most outrageous thing you've done to get your point across?

HER BINKY IS HER FRIEND

he American Academy of Pediatrics recommends stopping "binkies" at around 1 year of age. Some health care providers suggest that parents wean their children from the pacifier once they are mobile, to reduce the risk of fall-related injuries." ("Pacifiers: Introducing and Weaning." *Baby GooRoo.com*, updated 12 Feb 2021, https://babygooroo.com/articles/pacifiers-introducing-and-weaning.)

Really??

If this is the case, then we were really off track! My daughter sucked on her pacifier while pedaling her tricycle, painting murals, and playing chase in the park. She never had a 'fall-related binkie injury' and often resembled an eccentric artist with the paci perched on her lips instead of a cigarette.

Some of my mother friends were disturbed that their toddlers wanted comfort far beyond what grandparents and caretakers thought was appropriate. But by this time, I knew that everything with Mecca was a phase, and that this too would soon pass.

Around 2 ½ to 3 years old, my daughter started grinding her pacifiers to bits and silly me kept replenishing them. We could have bought shares of stock for the amount of money we spent on "bah-bahs" over the years.

One day I became fed up with binkies: I was done with replacing them, done with pawing sticky floors and dark alcoves to find them, done with washing guck and germs off them, just done!

"Mecca, I'm not going to take your pacifiers away, and I'm not going to try to make you stop using them, but I'm not going to buy anymore. You keep chewing them up so I think you're pretty finished with them. What you have is it. Okay?"

"Okay," she sadly agreed.

Well, just because I was complete, doesn't mean she was. For each paci she lost or misplaced, another magically appeared. She'd unearth them in sofa cushions, under beds, sandwiched between car seat cracks, beneath piles of clothes—freaking everywhere. I couldn't escape those things. She used her divine manifesting abilities to call forth three years' worth of abandoned soothers over a few months.

In the end, she contentedly weaned herself off her binky friend. There were no power struggles or arguments, no tears or tantrums. By the time she chomped the rubber nipple off the last one, she was ready to say goodbye to her comforting pal.

MY ATTEMPT AT CORPORAL PUNISHMENT

ne day I shared with another mother my recent frustration around grocery shopping which I had always kind of enjoyed. It was relaxing for me in a weird sort of way and I liked making up recipes in my head as I picked out food.

"Mecca's gotten into this thing where she climbs out of the basket every time we go shopping," I lamented about my 2-year-old daughter. "Or she grabs onto a ledge and pulls herself down the aisle in the cart like it's a ride at Disneyland, giggling all the way."

My friend laughed, although I didn't think my predicament was funny. "My boys used to do stuff like that. I just gave them a little pinch and they finally stopped."

"Oh, that really worked?"

"All the time," she said with the confidence of a mom who had already raised her kids.

I pondered my friend's suggestion—it sounded good when she said it, but didn't really sit right with me. I was definitely against spanking, and felt like pinching was probably in the same vein.

Growing up, I had been spanked, a lot. In fact, it was the popular form of punishment and control of kids in my community. Even today, I hear black parents threatening their kids with an "ass whooping" for any type of infraction, including talking back and eye rolling.

As a kid, I hated being punished, and spankings taught me to fear adults and authority, not respect, admire or trust them. I didn't buy into the adage of, "this hurts me more than it hurts you," while having my butt whipped, and I only grew better at hiding my exploits that might incur punishment.

As an adult dedicated to living spiritual principles and being a partner and guide for my daughter, spanking or hitting Mecca contradicted my beliefs. Hence, I felt trapped and exasperated—I was faced with an uncooperative child, and challenged by wanting to be in integrity with my values and overall commitment as a mom.

On our weekly trip to the supermarket, I hoped my daughter would behave and sit still long enough to shop quickly without any incidents. But she didn't. Her months of toddler gymnastics classes made her nimble enough to reach the shelves so swiftly I spent more time trying to corral her than picking out our food. She'd pull cans off the shelf before I could blink an eye, some landing in the back of the cart, some on the floor. I'd scramble to pick up the wreckage before a customer could trip or hurt themselves or before an employee busted my daughter for misconduct. My frustration finally overshadowed my principles... and I pinched her.

Just a slight squeeze on her chubby, delicious forearm—the one I loved to kiss and cuddle with—to get her to stop, to get her to listen, to make her understand I was serious, to make her stop laughing at my irritation.

"I. Said. Stop!"

She froze and scowled at me with disbelief in her squinted oval-shaped eyes. I had never intentionally tried to hurt her and she was shocked that I had pinched her.

Teary-eyed, fingers gripping the basket handle, she sat quietly while I finished shopping. I avoided looking at her sad, pouty face. I felt bad, but was pleased that my actions seemed to achieve my desired result. Later, I tried to rationalize my guilt away with thoughts like, *It was only a little nip...I didn't really hurt her*, neither of which made me feel any better.

The next time we went shopping, I was ready for anything. I had a defensive move in my playbook to allay any misbehavior on Mecca's part. *Bring it on!* I thought with unwarranted arrogance, and unresolved guilt.

When I glanced down at my grocery list, my daughter expertly reached over and grabbed a shelf ledge and pulled the cart closer so she could grasp the neatly stacked canned items once more. I asked her to stop, she ignored me. I moved the cart away from the tins, she tried to climb out, a sly smile on her face like she was egging me on. I pinched her, thinking I could control her behavior again with pain. I couldn't. She defiantly glared at me while pinching the back of my hand, hard! Twice as hard as I had pinched her.

"Ouch!" I said. My 2-year-old eyed me, daring me to do something about it.

We had a stare-off right in the middle of the grocery aisle; all customers disappeared into the background like townsfolk scattering before a gunfight. No one moved. My mind raced as I thought about what to do next. My fingers tapped an imaginary gun at my side.

Then, reason took over. Intuitively, I knew I was not going to win this battle. Her measures were totally lawful and justified—I had hurt her, she hurt me back. I was the one who had broken the Golden Rule first: do unto others as you would have them do unto you. Pinching her again would only lead to more unkind actions, the exact opposite of my intended teachings. I didn't want to create or perpetuate hostile behavior in my child which this minor corporal punishment had already done. I took a deep breath and relaxed my aggressive stance .

"I'm sorry I pinched you," I said. "This isn't cool, is it?"

She shook her head.

"I get so frustrated that you won't listen. You climbing out the cart and pulling things off the shelf makes it really difficult to shop."

Her face softened as she stared at me while I worked things out in my head.

"How about this?" I paused, looking for the right words. "Let's agree not to pinch or hurt each other anymore. Okay?"

She nodded. I hugged and kissed her and we continued shopping peacefully. I gathered our edibles as quickly as possible and left. Our moods were somber but at least we had come to an agreement.

This incident confirmed that my initial instincts had been correct, and that corporal punishment was not right for *my family*; I felt wrong hurting my child and didn't like my child hurting me. I was modeling the use of force and pain to control her, which she immediately turned against me.

After that day, I came up with other solutions to limit the accessibility of Mecca interrupting my shopping: I became better at managing grocery trips by leaving her at home with Thomas whenever possible, parking the cart in the center of the aisle far out of reach of potential enticements, and using carts with sturdy seat belts so she couldn't slip out so easily. I also learned to laugh at her antics which made them less irritating and her less prone to trying to aggravate me. Admittedly, she was pretty industrious; she could rock her legs and bend her torso, like on a swing, to propel a heavy shopping cart down a long grocery aisle. Had it been someone else's kid, I'd probably laugh hysterically at the sight of it too.

NO MORE MOMMY'S MILK

here's no one or right way to wean your baby from breastfeeding. I've known mothers to stop at a couple of months and some around pre-K. I had planned on nursing Mecca until her second birthday, but changed my mind to travel with my women's spiritual group to China. I was sorry to see our special bonding time come to an end, but after 9 months of pregnancy and 17 plus months of breastfeeding, I was ready to have my body back.

By this time Mecca was eating solids (organic homemade baby food) and our feedings were down to once a day before bedtime. About a month before I was going to end our nightly sessions, I started prepping Mecca for the change.

"Okay, Sweetie. Mommy's going to China in two months and I'd like to stop breastfeeding a couple of weeks before I leave," I explained to her.

I pulled out a calendar and pointed, "We're going to stop breastfeeding on this date, okay?" She looked at it curiously then tugged on my shirt for her nightly treat.

Because I had communicated intuitively with Mecca while in utero, I knew that on some level she understood what I was saying even though she couldn't answer back.

A couple of days later before we started our nightly session, I showed Mecca the circled date on the calendar and reminded her of what it meant. She glanced at it then began suckling my breast.

The week before our end date, I reminded Mecca a couple of times a day that we were ending our nightly breastfeeding soon. She'd look at me then return to whatever she was doing—usually playing with her toys or exploring the house.

On our final night, we sat together longer than usual relishing the last feeding. I chatted and caressed her head while she drank. When she finished, I said, "That's it Sweetie, no more Mommy's milk. We're done with this phase." She looked at me with warm, sleepy eyes then drifted off. I cradled her and reminisced about the wonderful experience of nursing my daughter. It had provided a delightful intimacy and trust I had never experienced.

At bedtime the next evening, Mecca pulled on my shirt to get some milk. I gently said, "No more milk, Honey. Remember last night was our last time." She looked at me as if thinking about our conversations, then let go of my shirt. No crying or pleading. She was content.

I pulled out her favorite books and read to her while she sat on my lap. I was a little disappointed to give up bonding through breastfeeding, but excited to begin a new chapter.

WHAT HAPPENED TO YOUR HAIR?

ne evening, I put my 3-year-old to bed as usual after storytime and went into my home office across the hall from her bedroom to catch up on a few things. I heard her get out of bed and move around her room, but I continued what I was doing since she hadn't called out for me. Then I heard her cutting something and figured she was playing with her scissors and paper.

"Mommy," she said as she stepped into my office.

I looked up and gasped loudly. My daughter had chopped off all of her hair with her toddler scissors. Her gorgeous curls were gone and replaced by a patchy one-inch mess in a matter of minutes. Her bright smile faded when she saw my alarm.

"What's going on?" Thomas yelled from the living room.

I was in shock. I couldn't answer. I gasped loudly again because words wouldn't form in my mouth.

"What's going on in there?" Thomas asked again.

Still, I couldn't speak.

I just put her to bed with a full head of hair, I thought, not fully comprehending what I was seeing.

Finally, Thomas came into the room to see why I wasn't responding. He looked at me with my glazed expression then looked at Mecca.

"Oh cool, you cut your hair off," he said so casually it knocked me out of my stupor.

"Your hair," was the best I could muster.

Thomas glided over to Mecca, picked her up and looked at her admiringly.

"You did this all by yourself?" he asked.

She nodded, beaming with pride.

"Now your hair looks like Mommy's," he said, looking at me. I had worn a buzz cut for years.

She grinned even bigger.

"Your hair?" I said. It was more of a question than a statement.

"I think it looks great!" Thomas said cheerfully, still holding her in his arms.

They both looked at me and waited for a response. I could tell I was failing miserably at reassuring her by their expectant expressions.

"Where's your beautiful hair?" I faltered.

"In there," she said, looking across the hall.

We walked into Mecca's bedroom and she pointed at the floor. Her luxurious curly brown locks were strewn across the floor like wind-blown leaves on a gusty day.

I held back my tears. It was upsetting seeing her hair clumped in patches on the carpet. I had spent countless hours washing it, combing it, and caring for it, just like I had her, and seeing it discarded on the floor was heartbreaking.

"I'm going to save it," I said and went to get a large plastic baggie.

Thomas and Mecca watched in disbelief as I crawled on the floor scooping up handfuls of hair and shoving them into the baggie.

"Why is Mommy doing that?" I heard my daughter ask him.

"Why don't you just throw it away?" Thomas asked me.

"I don't know."

"What are you going to do with it?"

"I don't know but I just can't throw it away like useless garbage."

It was blatantly apparent I was the only one concerned with collecting Mecca's hair off the flooring. Neither offered to help me. They stood for a moment before Thomas tucked her back in bed and headed out. I finally finished, kissed her goodnight and exited her room, clutching a baggie stuffed with her butchered locks.

"What's the big deal? It's just hair," Thomas said back in our bedroom. This coming from a bald man.

"Yeah, but it was beautiful hair, and now it's gone."

"Well, it was her hair and she cut it off. It was her choice. She probably wanted her hair to look like yours."

"Maybe," I sighed.

"You need to say something to her. She looks up to you and you weren't very nice."

"I'll talk to her in the morning," I replied.

During the night I contemplated my despair—I had so many feelings swirling through me to sort out: was I pissed off because my daughter had cut her hair, or just sad to see it gone? Was I worried people would think I chopped off my daughter's hair to look like mine? I remembered that at eight years old I had cut off my hair and had been teased for having such a short style. Also, people had often mistook me for a boy, which really angered me. I didn't want either of those for my child. This upheaval of thoughts and emotions erupted as my daughter stood in front of me with an uneven blotchy haircut from a dull pair of toddler scissors.

I resolved to make peace with my concerns as I went to sleep that night. Thomas was right, I hadn't been very nice to Mecca and it was her hair. She'd have to live with it.

By morning I had my senses back. I determined my upset had more to do with my experience as a child, my fear of people being mean to her, and also a feeling of loss for the hair I had so lovingly cared for. To me, it was a part of her that was now gone.

I went to Mecca's bedroom to talk to her. "I'm sorry I reacted so poorly last night. I was quite surprised when you walked into my office and didn't know what to say. I'm sorry if I made you feel bad." I hugged her tightly and kissed her cheek. She squeezed me back.

I held her at arm's length scrutinizing her tufts. "Well, if you're going to have short hair, we've got to style it so it's cute," I said smiling at her.

She nodded.

"It's pretty uneven. Can I shape it up for you?"

"Okay."

She climbed onto a chair and I trimmed her hair so that it was all one length (about half an inch or so). I wet it and slicked it back with gel until it was very stylish and hip. She beamed in the mirror, and I was actually quite pleased with the result.

Within a few days, I took Mecca to get her ears pierced. She'd been asking for earrings, but I had been reluctant thinking they might get pulled out while she played. I changed my mind because I was afraid she'd be mistaken for a boy and happily took her to the mall.

"Which color do you want?" Her eyes glistened as she looked at the selection of earrings to choose from at the store. She had waited a long time for this moment and was thrilled that she was finally getting her ears pierced.

"Those," she said, pointing to a pair of rose-colored starter studs.

"Pretty! Okay, it's going to hurt a bit." I said. "You ready?"

She nodded. The clerk cleaned, marked, and pierced her ears without too many tears. As soon as Mecca saw herself in the mirror with her brand-new studs, her face lit up like a Christmas tree. We grabbed lunch and celebrated this rite of passage.

I was surprised that everyone loved her new short style. She was very happy with it until a few weeks later when she asked me to put her hair in a ponytail.

"I'm sorry Honey, your hair is not long enough. You'll have to wait until it grows out before you can have a ponytail again."

"Oh," she said, pouting. I embraced my daughter and reassured her she would have a ponytail once more.

I wouldn't have cut her curls so close, but I must admit, it was much easier caring for her shorter hair—and it was kind of cool that we rocked similar hairdos.

ICE BREAKERS:

Parents: What would you do if your child cut off their hair?

Kids: Do you think it's okay to cut off your own hair without talking to your parents first?

SHE WON'T MEDITATE WITH ME ANYMORE

used to think it was so cool that my 3-year-old daughter would sit and meditate with me. Well, it was more like she would close her eyes, sit with her legs crossed and her palms facing up on her lap with thumbs to index fingers. I didn't brag about it, but I felt a lot of self-satisfaction. She could sit quietly for several minutes before getting bored and leaving.

I really thought she was embracing our spiritual practices and was well on her way to becoming a child Buddha. I envisioned her leading children's meditation classes.

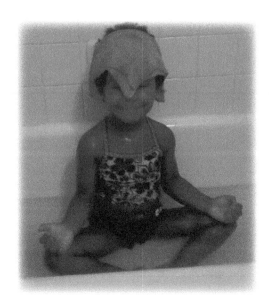

The first time Mecca said she didn't want to meditate was no big deal. But after numerous requests, and several refusals on her part, I was disappointed. I felt like I had failed in some way. My inflated ego was crushed and wanted to figure out a way to get her to sit with me again. Not very spiritual, I know, but sometimes it's like that.

Since we have raised Mecca to make her own choices, I knew I needed to get over my discontent. Trying to force her to do anything wasn't going to work, and surely wasn't going to make her any more enlightened.

So, I asked for guidance and clarity about the situation during meditation one day. Boy did I receive a crystal-clear message from above:

> *"Leave her alone! You meditate to feel connected to your spiritual self. She is already aware of her connection and doesn't need to meditate to get there."*

With this new understanding, I stopped making her disinterest in meditating mean a rejection of me and my spiritual practices, and began honoring her process. Good thing I did, because she wasn't going to meditate with me anyway.

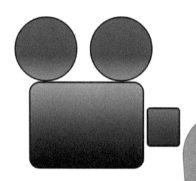

Difference Between Mom vs. Dad Communication

Thomas, "Okay, now she just used like 500 words to explain how she was reviewing our daughter's competition and that's very typical of a female. Generally, now a male tends to be more direct and use fewer words and so that was just my style in trying to get over the hump of the seriousness of the event."

Link: https://youtu.be/bbu75jBT_wI

SHE'S BEING SO MEAN TO ME

s we walked into our favorite deli to grab dinner, my 3-year-old was being mean to me—she wouldn't take my hand, wouldn't look at me, and wouldn't talk to me. Mecca and I hadn't spent time together in days because of my busy work schedule, so I was disappointed that our evening wasn't going well.

* * *

For over a year, I had been the On-Air Fundraising Producer for a public television station. I was in charge of producing live and pre-recorded local pledge breaks for our fundraising campaigns ("pledge drives"). I loved my job! I got to work with talented, creative and professional on-air talent, production crew members, volunteers, and staff. I was an independent contractor with flexible hours and the ability to work from home when needed. Prior to taking this position, I had been Mecca's full-time caregiver. I hadn't planned on going back to work, but I started volunteering at the station and ended up being offered a job because of my experience and background; it was a perfect fit for me and the organization.

Before I started my new position, Thomas and I agreed that Mecca would be taken care of by both of us; we weren't going to put her in daycare. He was self-employed and had a small home repair and remodeling business that he would work in the early/late mornings while I took care of our daughter. Then, we would switch off, and I'd go to work in the afternoons and evenings. Some days I only worked for four hours, but once a pledge drive was in full swing, my days could easily extend to 14 hours or more. However, I was home in the mornings to take care of my daughter and often made it back to tuck her in and do storytime. Mecca spent ample time with us participating in various activities like gymnastics, art days at the museum, play dates at the zoo, and even meeting new friends on her excursions with Daddy.

Our co-parenting routine and scheduling had worked seamlessly until this particular pledge drive. The new upper management team extended the fund-raising campaign from two weeks to three weeks and added several live morning shifts which I had to produce. I now had to work mornings, afternoons, and evenings while Thomas took care of Mecca on his own. This was not what we had agreed to, but he was being a trooper and my daughter hadn't complained. We knew the pledge drive would end and I'd be done with the grueling schedule, so we sucked it up and dealt with it; even when at one point I hadn't seen Mecca in three days because she was asleep when I left in the morning, and was asleep when I returned home late at night. What was supposed to have been a part-time gig had turned into a massive undertaking.

One evening, Thomas and Mecca stopped by the control room while I was working.

"Mecca wanted to show you her skateboard," Thomas said as she excitedly held up her new wheels.

"Skateboard?" I raised my eyebrows. "When did you start skateboarding?" I asked her.

"A couple of days ago," she said.

"I didn't know that." I could feel my throat tightening and tears forming. "Nobody told me."

"You were working," Thomas said. It was a simple statement of truth that stung like a belly-flop from the high dive, because I felt guilty for not being around.

"You bought her a skateboard without telling me?" It was a question and an accusation.

"No, she found it in the movie the-
atre parking lot," he said.

"Oh, that's an odd place to find
a skateboard," I said. "Do you know
how to ride it?" I asked my daughter.

"No."

"She just started practicing with
it," Thomas added.

"I used to love my skateboard," I said absently to no one in particular.

I turned away to slyly wipe my eyes so they wouldn't see me cry. I was sad
and hurt that I had missed this moment in her life. Fortunately, we were in the
back of the room and on a break so most of the crew was getting food, not
paying attention to us.

"You guys want to grab something to eat? There's food set up in the volunteer
room," I said, looking from one to the other hoping they would hang out with
me for a while.

Mecca glanced up at Thomas. "No, we're going home. We've been out all
day," he said. "We just stopped by to say hello and show you her skateboard."

"Oh, okay. You sure?"

"Yeah."

I walked them to the elevator. The bell chimed and I kissed them goodbye. I
tried to look upbeat while my heart ached. Thomas took Mecca's hand and led
her in. She leaned close to him. He held the bulky skateboard in his other hand,
the place where my palm would usually be. Mecca lifted her fingers to wave
as the doors closed between us, leaving me alone on the opposite side of the
chasm.

I stood reflectively by the elevator before returning to work. I felt left out
and separate from my family, a new and uncomfortable position for me. I had
always been there as mom, caregiver, nurturer, teacher; but now my daughter
was growing up without me. Her life continued with Thomas while I worked.

I realized I wouldn't get any 'do-overs' or 'first times' if I wasn't present—even with something as simple as seeing her ride a skateboard for the first time.

Finally, I pulled myself out of the haze, stuffed my emotions inside and went back to the control room; I had a job to do and responsibilities to fulfill.

A couple of days later, I was at the entrance of a deli demanding my 3-year-old hold my hand, like she had always done, happily and willingly.

"Mecca, come here!" She bolted through the restaurant door as I opened it.

"No!" She snapped and ran ahead of me.

I caught her and clutched her hand, which she immediately snatched back. It was unlike her to run ahead, and out of character for her to pull away.

"Well, if you're going to be mean we can just go home now!" I was instantly frustrated and already exhausted from working too many hours. Thomas had dropped Mecca off at my job so we could spend time together. She had colored and watched videos in my cubicle while I finished up and I hadn't noticed that she was cranky.

She stared at me blankly.

Oh, come on! Really? I just want to have a quick dinner and go home, I thought to myself.

I glanced down at my miserable child and realized this was going to get uglier if I didn't shift my attitude and demeanor—my frustration with her was quickly escalating the situation.

I took a deep breath and thought for a moment before bending down to look in my daughter's eyes.

"Are you mad at Mommy because I've been working so much?"

My little one burst out crying. I pulled her into my arms, hugged her tightly and just let her bawl. I finally picked her up, moved out of the entrance to the restaurant and found a booth for us to sit in.

"I'm sorry I haven't been around lately," I blubbered through my own tears. "I know this is not the agreement we all had," my own guilt and sadness busting through like a dam failure flooding a village.

She sobbed louder. I wept as I organized my thoughts. People walked by and stared briefly, but left us alone.

"I will take care of this. I have another month left on my contract, so I can't just leave my job, but I will handle this. I promise I will be around to take care of you again. Is that okay?" She nodded and continued to whimper.

We sat there, holding each other and crying, until we were both done. We finally wiped our tear-streaked faces, blew our snotty noses, ordered dinner and ate in silence.

By the time I arrived home, I was clear about my next steps.

"I'm not going to renew my contract next month," I told Thomas.

"Why?" he asked, surprised, but probably a bit relieved since I hadn't been around.

I told him about my evening with Mecca, crying at the deli, and the promise I made her.

"I'm sorry. I know you really enjoyed your job."

"Yeah, I did. But it's changed a lot since the new management came in. This isn't what I signed up for. My relationship with Mecca has suffered, and I haven't kept up my end of our agreement to co-parent. It's not worth it," I shook my head in dismay.

"Well, it's totally up to you. You can work or not work. I'll be fine, we'll be fine."

"Thanks Honey." I kissed him goodnight, checked on Mecca and went to bed.

Within a week, I informed my boss of my decision. She wasn't surprised given how the pledge drive had changed and my hours had increased so dramatically. Also, she liked my daughter and understood my commitment to raising her. When I had volunteered, I often brought Mecca with me, so most of the staff knew her.

Once I gave my notice, I felt relieved and sad at the same time. Relieved because I could regain my integrity as a mom, wife and participating member of my family; sad, because I had loved producing and would miss the fun and excitement of it.

* * *

Mecca remained chilly for a few days after our incident at the deli. When she finally hugged me again, I knew I had absolutely made the right choice—nothing was worth losing my happy, loving daughter. I knew I could always work in the future, but she would never, ever, be 3 years old again.

THAT'S MY CHILD ON THE FLOOR

enox Square is a lively mall to people watch in Atlanta. It's very fashionable and attracts a wide variety of clientele: hipsters, plain-janes, wealthy and wannabes. We'd go there frequently to meander indoors, getting out of the heat or cold, and to have lunch or sit at the coffee bar gawking at the crowd. Basically, we'd make a day of it.

This Saturday afternoon was particularly crowded—lots of families with kids and groups milled around.

Mecca loved to make the long trek from the parking structure to our favorite eatery at the opposite end of the mall. At 2 years old, she preferred to walk like a big girl rather than ride in her stroller. Thomas held her hand as I sauntered ahead, popping in and out of stores and window shopping, enjoying my freedom of not being totally responsible for her at that moment.

When I reached the café where we had planned to eat lunch, I realized I had lost them. I waited a moment before retracing my steps down the bustling corridor. I didn't think they were too far behind me so I browsed as I walked.

Hmm, sounds like some kid is having a tantrum, I mused as I approached a loud noise.

As I got closer to the ruckus, I saw Thomas casually standing in the walkway staring down at the floor. I followed his gaze...*Oh man, that's Mecca on the floor!*

I was paralyzed—*should I intervene or run the other way?*

Bystanders walked by glaring at my daughter flailing on the ground. A full-blown tantrum was in progress: screaming, crying, arms and legs thrashing about. Some shook their heads in disgust, others just laughed and kept on going. One young man was courteous enough to point her out to his friends, shake his head and smirk.

I looked back up at Thomas, he was totally unaffected by her tantrum and his audience. He was giving Mecca space and freedom to express her emotions without being embarrassed or angry.

Observing that he had the situation completely under control, I quickly turned and scurried back to our meeting place before being spotted by either one of them. I really didn't feel like dealing with a tantrum in the middle of a busy mall on one of my few days off from being full-time mom.

A few minutes later, I spotted Thomas and Mecca ambling toward me. He was holding her hand and calmly walking at her pace. For the most part, Mecca looked pretty good considering she was just flailing on the ground. Her eyes were still red and a bit puffy, but the tears had stopped streaming and snot wasn't running out her nose.

"You guys ready to eat?" I asked as they approached.

"Yep!" said Thomas.

"You okay Mecca?" she nodded.

We ordered lunch, then Thomas filled me in on their last few minutes. I listened intently before admitting I had fled the scene. We laughed and ended up having a lovely afternoon.

After that day, Mecca lost interest in throwing tantrums. I guess she figured they're only fun when someone reacted to them, and it was clear that at least her daddy wouldn't.

THAT'S MY CHILD ON THE FLOOR, PART 2: THE EXORCIST & THE BUDDHA

WRITTEN BY THOMAS KELLER

ave you ever watched a child throwing an outrageous tantrum in a public place and wondered what could create such horrible behavior?

My judgment day came when my wife, our 2-year-old daughter, and I traveled to Lenox Square, a favorite place for us to escape the heat and humidity of Atlanta in the summer. Lenox is the heart of Atlanta's stylish, upwardly mobile world, filled with people of diversity and perfect for people-watching and being watched.

From day one my daughter has been strong-willed, so when she decided to walk, I held her hand as we began our hike from the parking lot to Panera Bread for lunch. Entering the mall, we descended the long escalator into a massive swarm of humanity. My wife took advantage of her freedom from childcare by quickly walking ahead window shopping with childlike awe in her eye and a skip in her step. My walk slowed to a crawl as my daughter and I weaved our way through the masses from one end of the mall toward the other.

I don't know what set my daughter off. Maybe it was my refusal to stop at the intoxicating smell of baking chocolate chip cookies at Starbucks. But she decided it was "go" time, and within seconds, she was wailing on the floor on her back as if possessed by a demon in some Exorcist movie. She was screaming at siren level, arms and legs thrashing about like worms exposed to the sunlight from underground.

The flood of people in the mall parted as if we were Moses at the Red Sea. They continued to walk around us, many aghast, others amazed, a few concerned. Then a miracle happened. As quickly as my daughter collapsed, I became possessed by the Buddha. A warm feeling of calmness and quiet infused my body. I stood over her protecting her from the crowds, in love with her. I didn't say a word. There were no pleas for her to stop it, to knock it off. I wasn't ashamed, embarrassed, or indifferent. I just stood there in love. I was clear that I was willing to go through this with her as long as she wanted to, and that I was not interested in conceding to the demonic behavior.

I also knew I would not let any "well-meaning person" interfere, and nobody attempted to. I don't remember if our possessions went on for 3 seconds, 3 minutes or 3 hours, but at some point, she changed her mind and relaxed. I put my hand down to help her up, brushed her off, wiped her eyes and we resumed our walk to Panera Bread to meet my wife for lunch. There was no judgment from me, no lessons for me to impart.

I don't remember meeting my wife at the café, but she said that we did and that we had a fine lunch together. Regardless of how the rest of my parenting record appears, I will forever have my Golden Buddha moment. Oh, and my daughter never chose that behavior again.

4-7 YEARS

HOMESCHOOLING 201—LEARNING TO READ

hadn't planned on teaching Mecca how to read until she was six or seven years old because I had come across articles about the Danish educational system where kids in Denmark learn to read later than American children, but have a much higher literacy rate. According to these articles, children's brains are more developed at seven and it's easier for them to learn and comprehend at this age. But all that changed when my daughter asked me to teach her to read around 4 ½ years old.

Since I thought I had plenty of time before this phase, I wasn't prepared. I was still enjoying our nightly storytime and believed that would continue for a few more years. Nevertheless, Mecca wanted to read, so I scrambled to find a technique or system that taught reading. However, none of the methods resonated with me, therefore I pulled from various sources, then used my intuition and came up with approaches on my own.

We did most of our activities on the floor in my small, neat home office/guest room in order to spread out. Mecca's room was far too messy and busy to study in. She had clothes and toys strewn across every square inch of her bedroom and it was impossible to concentrate in there. She would also get sidetracked fidgeting with a gadget or flipping through her colorful books.

My office was quite comfortable and conducive for learning. It had a small pull-out couch, end table, armoire and floor pillow. We sat on the carpet and drew on the dry erase board that leaned against the wall. Sometimes Mecca would curl up on the comfy floor pillow while we did our lessons. She often laid upside down looking backward at the board while identifying letters and numbers and liked to recite lyrics to her favorite songs from this position.

In addition to writing on the board, we also used flashcards and sang the alphabet song to help her memorize the order of the letters. It was amusing to scatter the cards on the floor and watch her put them in the correct sequence while singing together. She learned quickly which required me to stay creative to hold her interest.

Once she had learned letters, I figured it was time to teach her words. I wanted to make learning as entertaining as possible so we played Hangman, that old game where a person has to guess the letters in a word before the stick figure is hanged. I started with simple two, three and four letter words that she used in everyday language, such as *it, he, me, mom, dad, cat, dog, food, and home*. She'd guess a letter then eagerly wait to see if I drew a body part on the diagram or filled in the blanks for the word. I wanted her to win, hence I rarely 'hanged' her. I would draw in ears and eyes and even eyebrows until she guessed all the correct letters for the word. We'd chuckle at my silly pictures then play more rounds. She also used the flashcards to form simple words. They were easy to pick up and arrange and rearrange into different sequences.

A game we still play today as a family in the car is to name words that start with the letter '___'. If the letter was 'p', Mecca would name off all the words she could think of that started with a 'p'. It was exciting to see how far she could go. At first, she may have gotten less than 10 words, then it expanded to 20 and 30 and so on. We were often surprised at the number of words she could come up with in one session.

Teaching Mecca to read was my inauguration into being her homeschool educator. Now, I was not only Mom, but I was also "Responsible for providing intellectual, moral, and social instructions," according to an article by educator Robert Peters, (Peters, Robert. "The Difference Between a Teacher and an Educator." *Medium.com*, 20 March 2017, https://medium.com/@robertpeters/the-difference-between-a-teacher-and-an-educator-2ac6392a1e43.) that distinguished the difference between educator and teacher. As such, I became frustrated when my daughter started doing headstands and acrobatics during our lessons. She'd toss the floor pillow aside, lean her head and back against the wall, then push her legs up until she was upright. She would hold this position as long as possible while I sat at the dry erase board stunned at her behavior.

"Aah, what are you doing?" I asked.

"Practicing my headstands."

"I can see that. But it's study time now. You can practice your gymnastics later," I said.

"Go ahead. I'm listening," she said.

"Please stop."

"I'm listening."

I'd ask her a question to prove she wasn't concentrating, but she usually had the correct answer. Yet and still, I was irritated by her constant wiggling. I felt like she wasn't taking me or her lessons seriously. I even wondered if she'd be labeled hyperactive or difficult if she was in a classroom, or if I had started her too early since my original plan had been to follow the Danish educational model.

As we moved to short phrases and multisyllabic words, her squirming increased and she moved to the middle of the room away from where I sat. We still played hangman, however I would separate the blank dashes with slashes to indicate a different word or syllable.

"Okay Hon. This word has three syllables." I would then draw _ _/_ _ _/_ _ _, for al/pha/bet, on the board before she started guessing the letters. It was a great way for her to integrate auditory and visual learning by sounding out words while seeing them written out.

"A," she said from a standing bridge pose.

"Can you please come over here by the board," I asked.

"I want to do it from here," she insisted. "I can see."

I rolled my eyes and filled in the blanks. She smiled smugly and repositioned herself.

Mecca enjoyed learning to read and I liked teaching her, aside from the unorthodox calisthenics; I didn't know any other kids that studied like they were in a P.E. class. For the most part, I took my lesson cues by observing my daughter. When I noticed her singing Justin Bieber songs repeatedly, I printed out the lyrics, cut them up and had her piece them together like a puzzle, all while listening to his CD in the background. We'd sing, dance and work. If she got stuck, I'd rewind the song over and over so she could hear the lyrics, then she'd find the verse amongst the cut-up pieces. She was thrilled when she finally organized a few verses then followed them as she sang.

We rarely studied more than an hour or so a day, but she progressed pretty quickly. We incorporated all that she learned into our nightly storytime. I'd have her identify words and try to read passages. We sat side by side on my office couch taking turns holding books on our laps reading to each other.

I expected Mecca's tumbling to cease as she got older, but it only ramped up. I felt like I was corralling puppies trying to get my daughter to remain seated. She'd go in the opposite direction of where I wanted her to focus. Occasionally though, she would acquiesce and squat quietly in the center of the room, attentively with her head cocked, for a moment, until my back was turned, then hunch into a backbend or drop into splits.

"You know, if you were in school, you'd have to sit at a desk and pay attention," I tried to sound threatening.

"But I'm not in school."

"Hmph! Why can't you just sit still? You're driving me crazy with all your moving." I waved my arms in frustration.

"I don't know," she hunched her shoulders. "I like to move around."

"But you're not paying attention."

"Yes I am."

This went on for weeks. Trying to make my daughter stay in place only created tension between us and delayed our lessons. I was completely baffled—her actions appeared like she was unfocused and inattentive, yet she constantly proved her awareness by answering easily and quickly from her contorted positions. I felt stuck. I talked to my husband about it, but he didn't have a solution either.

Then, one day, Thomas excitedly told me about an interview he heard with the author of a book called *Smart Moves: Why Learning Is Not All in Your Head* by Carla Hannaford, Ph.D. He said this book talked about how kids learn and thought it might support me with Mecca. I ordered it immediately. I was desperate to understand my daughter's behavior—when I was in school, we sat quietly at our desks and listened to our teachers (or at least pretended to listen); we didn't do acrobatics in class.

This book changed my life! I skimmed the pages looking for help. Bam! I found exactly what I needed in Chapter 6, Movement. Hannaford writes:

> "Movement integrates and anchors new information and experience in our neural networks. And movement is vital to all actions by which we embody and express our learning, our understanding and ourselves" (Hannaford 107.)

The more I read, the more I relaxed. You may wonder how a few sentences can be life-changing. Well, I realized that my daughter was not hyperactive, or unable to concentrate, or being disrespectful of my time and efforts, but was simply anchoring in all that she learned as she balanced, twisted and flexed on the floor. This was why she answered my questions quickly and progressed in her reading, even when I thought she wasn't paying attention or taking me seriously.

I also recognized a couple of other things: as Mecca's lessons increased in complexity, her movement increased to make it easier for her to anchor in the complex information she was learning; therefore, it was unrealistic of me to think she would squirm less as she aged. Additionally, I had been so locked into how I thought studying should look based on my upbringing, education, and societal norms that I was making my kid wrong for not abiding by my standards. Fortunately, I found the *Smart Moves* book and shifted my perspective before I quelled her desire and enthusiasm to learn. We were homeschooling after all, like she reminded me, thereby it was impractical to worry about future scenarios of her being instructed to remain seated in a classroom with 20 other kids.

From that point on, I didn't ask Mecca to sit still. I happily wrote on the dry erase board and let her move freely around the room learning to read words, phrases and sentences while standing on her head or launching into a backbend.

ICE BREAKERS:

Kids: Is it easier for you to learn if you move around a bit?

How Do You Handle Your Child's Disappointment?

Sandra, "Then I started trying to figure out what can I do to make her feel better? Like it's my responsibility to make her feel better...I think the problem with that is one, I don't let her develop any muscles that she needs to be able to be disappointed and then bring herself out of it because everybody goes through some disappointments, some failures, some tough times, and then two, when I start parenting from being over accommodating I don't think I'm being a powerful parent."

Link: https://youtu.be/f_qO0EsMM-Y

A BAD DAY FOR MY 6-YEAR-OLD

s I tucked Mecca in one night, she blurted out, "This was the fifth worst day ever!"

I raised my eyebrows—I thought we had had a nice day. My body tensed as I mentally scanned our activities to figure out what had caused my daughter so much distress. We were temporarily living on the east coast of the island of Oahu, in Hawaii, in the quaint, friendly town of Kailua. I homeschooled Mecca while Thomas worked part-time on the island doing home repairs. We spent most days in the sun having fun and exploring the beauty and magnificence of our surroundings. Life was pretty good.

"Why?" I asked.

She actually had a list. "Well, first when I went to the pool today, Daddy wouldn't get in the water with me because it was too cold."

"Oh."

"Then, when we were at the beach for the event, I was cold and it drizzled a little on me," she said.

"Really?"

"And, I was really cold on the bus ride home."

"Hmm. I'm sorry you had such a bad day," I said to her sad, pouty face. "I'm sure tomorrow will be better."

"Yeah," she said with a slight moan.

I kissed her goodnight and left the room. My shoulders relaxed as I thought about how blessed we are that the above constituted a bad day for my daughter. She wasn't starving or neglected or sickly or abused or living in danger like many unfortunate children in the world. Thomas and I had created a loving, safe environment for her to flourish in. So, I decided, we were doing a pretty good job if this was the fifth worst day for Mecca. What was her worst day ever you may wonder? She didn't say, but I've never seen her as upset as the first (and last) time we woke her up to eat in the hospital when she was a newborn.

A BEDTIME ALARM?

"Why does Mecca's alarm go off at 12:45 at night?" my mom asked one evening while visiting us from out of state.

"So she can go to bed. Otherwise, she would be up all night," I said.

"I've never heard of such a thing. Why is a 4-year-old up so late?"

"Because she's not sleepy."

I really wasn't trying to be a smartass with my mom, but I found it difficult to explain my reasoning for letting my child stay up past what most people considered a normal bedtime.

Let's backtrack a bit. I used to relish the days when I would put Mecca to bed around 9:00, then bake my store-bought chocolate chip cookies and kick back on my couch in my serene, comfy home office. I'd exhale from the busy day and enjoy the quiet time and my sweet treat.

Unlike most kids, my daughter stopped taking naps around 2 years old. She just wasn't sleepy and I finally gave up struggling to make her lie down. This also meant no break for me in the middle of the day to breathe or catch up on things, so bedtime was my respite.

Then at around 3 years old, Mecca started getting out of bed after storytime to play in her room before settling in for the night. I could hear her talking to her dolls or pretending to read her books—she was quite busy moving around in there. She was as wide awake as I was, but I continued to put her back in bed because that seemed like the logical thing to do, even though she said she wasn't tired. Besides, I didn't know any other kids that stayed up past 10:00pm.

Eventually, I began dreading our once pleasant bedtime ritual. Each night was a fight to get her to sleep. I'd tuck her in and she'd get out of bed as soon as I left her room. I was irritated and irritable. Since Thomas was usually asleep by 10:00, he missed all of the commotion.

I became so tired of fighting with her, I decided to let her self-regulate and go to bed when she wanted. That was a disaster. She'd be up after I went to bed at 1:00am, then sleep until midafternoon, which meant I was waiting for her to wake up before we could go anywhere. And, I was missing my work-out time at the gym, or cutting it short because I felt guilty getting her up.

I finally admitted my struggle to Thomas one night while we were chatting in our bedroom and Mecca was in her room playing.

"I've been having a hard time getting Mecca to bed," I wearily confessed.

"What's going on?"

"Well, she's not tired. We do storytime, I tuck her in, then she gets out of bed. I put her back to bed and she gets out. Or she'll stay in her crib and cry out or make some other loud, obnoxious noise. I'm sick of fighting with her all night."

"What are you thinking?"

"Letting her stay up until I go to bed at one."

He frowned and his voice harshened. "I don't think so. She doesn't need to be up that late. She's a kid and needs sleep. No."

I wasn't surprised by his response and had mentally prepared for it. I took a deep breath before I answered.

"You're more than welcome to put her to bed. I'll read her a story then you can fight with her to go to sleep. If you're lucky, you can probably get her settled by midnight."

"I go to work. I'm not up that late."

"Yep, I know. That's why you've missed all the drama."

"What is she doing all night?" he asked.

"Playing with her dolls, her books, her markers, cutting paper."

"I don't know. That seems really late."

"Yeah, it is. But if she's not tired, then she's not tired."

It took a few days for Thomas to get on board with letting Mecca stay up until 1:00am, but since I was the one caring for her all day, he finally conceded. And he definitely didn't want to battle putting her to bed each night.

Now that Thomas and I were in agreement, I had to come up with an action plan. The hardest part for me was setting boundaries with my daughter about my nighttime availability. I didn't want to be on 'Mommy duty' all night just because she wanted to stay up late, so I figured out guidelines that would support both of us:

- ✓ After storytime, you can play quietly in your room until bedtime, but no electronics.
- ✓ If you need help with a project, find something else you can do on your own.
- ✓ Ask for a snack <u>before</u> storytime.
- ✓ Pretend like I'm not home. Don't come looking for me wanting to hang out.
- ✓ If we have plans in the morning, you'll have to get up.
- ✓ You'll have to wake up three times a week to go to the gym with me.
- ✓ Set your alarm clock for 12:45am, with the snooze button on, so you'll have time to stop whatever you're doing, brush your teeth, use the bathroom and get in bed by 1:00am.
- ✓ *If you become a cranky and unpleasant child, you'll have to go to bed earlier.*

I can't say that my so-called guidelines were strictly adhered to, but at least I had a benchmark to reach for. I often gave in and got her a snack after storytime and sometimes hung out with her. However, letting her self-regulate her bedtime immediately decreased our nighttime drama. Both of us were much happier, and I made sure she had plenty of days to sleep in as late as she wanted, so she didn't become that cranky and unpleasant child. Hence, when my mother had asked me about Mecca's late-night alarm clock, I didn't even know where to begin the saga.

ICE BREAKERS:

Parents: How would you handle a child who's naturally a night owl?

Kids: How do you feel being forced to go to bed before you're tired?

SOMETIMES YOU JUST HAVE TO DO WHAT WE ASK

pontaneous road trips are oftentimes the best kind—unexpected adventures with little time to think or plan. At the last minute, I arranged a weekend rafting trip to celebrate Father's Day. I was compelled to do something extra special for Thomas and thought he would enjoy this. I found a family-friendly excursion in the idyllic mountains of North Carolina, a short three-hour drive from bustling Atlanta.

Thomas and Mecca had never been whitewater rafting. I'd gone a couple of times and had loved the rush of speeding down wild slushing rapids. Because this was a family-friendly tour, the rapids were mild, but the river was frigid.

We shrieked and chuckled while rafting on the first day. About halfway through the trip, the guide paddled to the tranquil bank to allow the group to swim in the frosty water if we wanted. Feeling bold, we took a bracing dip in the freezing stream, then quickly dried off and warmed up on a huge sundrenched boulder. We had a blast river-rafting, but wanted a different experience for the second day and decided to try tubing instead. We rented three oversized black rubber tubes with sturdy handles on top.

"You need to wear your lifejacket," I said to Mecca as we prepared to launch into the chilly water.

"Why?" my 7-year-old asked, pointing to adults, teens, and tweens leisurely floating down the stream. "No one else has one on."

"They're older than you," said Thomas.

"I don't like wearing them," she whined. "They're uncomfortable and they don't fit right."

"You still have to wear it," I said. "The water is moving much faster than it looks and if you fall in it can be hard to get out."

"You could get swept down the river in no time," Thomas added.

"I surfed in Hawaii and I'm a strong swimmer. I'm a better swimmer than you," she argued, looking at me. Thomas was a former lifeguard and could easily outswim both of us.

"Maybe you are," I said with more attitude than intended, "But you've never been tubing and you don't know what it's like to fall into a rushing cold river."

"But…" she continued her protest.

Thomas and I looked at each other and said in unison, "Put the lifejacket on!" Mecca sighed and begrudgingly put the vest on.

We launched from the wide-mouthed river into the frigid water. Huge boulders and lush trees surrounded the wading pool-like entry. We watched other tubers ahead of us to gage the strength and direction of the current. Thomas tethered Mecca's tube to his with an old rope and we laughed and screamed as we careened down the swooshing river, narrowly avoiding rocks and other tubers. It was so much fun we ran back up to the launch area to do the three-quarter mile trip again.

On our second run, I got out of my tube half way through our ride to get the car so I could drive down and pick up Thomas and Mecca at the end. By this time, we were exhausted and didn't want to trek back up the hill to our vehicle.

I leisurely changed my clothes and dried off my gear before heading down. I thought I had timed it perfectly to see them float down the river, but I waited and waited and waited. I recognized tubers that had been alongside us gliding by, so I knew something had delayed them.

I paced and lingered anxiously at the bank. Deep breathing helped mollify my agitation. More tubers drifted by. I wanted to shout out, *Have you seen my family?* but they were too far away. I felt helpless standing at the shore with nothing to do but focus on my breath to calm down. I couldn't walk or drive around the winding river to find them because there were no trails or roads on the rim.

Finally, they rounded the bend. Mecca was hunched over in her tube, arms wrapped around her knees, shaking and teary-eyed—my heart sank as I ran to the edge to meet them.

"What took you guys so long?" I yelled, reaching to help them out of the water.

"Mecca got knocked into the river," Thomas said.

"Mommy," she said as I pulled her out of her tube. I hugged her tightly while she cried.

"What happened? I barely left you guys."

"I'm, I'm cold," she shivered and dug deeper into me.

"Her tube hit a rock and she flew off into the river," Thomas explained. "I scooped her up by her lifejacket as she sped by me."

"I hate tubing," Mecca mumbled through tears.

I soothed her as she burrowed into me. "Are you hurt or just scared?"

"Scared," she shuddered. We held each other as she calmed down before loading their gear into the trunk. Once on the road the tension eased and we all relaxed.

I tried my best not to say it because I knew I was being a smartass and maybe even a bit insensitive, but I just couldn't help myself.

"Good thing you had that life vest on, Miss 'I'm a better swimmer than you'." I shook my head and shoulders in a mocking way.

Mecca glared at me and growled. She wasn't amused at all and certainly didn't like hearing "I told you so."

ALLOWANCE-TO GIVE OR NOT TO GIVE

hen I was a kid, I received a weekly allowance for the chores I performed around the house. A couple of dollars went pretty far back then. I could buy candy and the little trinkets that I wanted.

So, after reading a very informative article about the do's and don'ts of modern-day allowances, I began thinking it was time for my 7-year-old to learn how to manage money—it's never too early to see how far a dollar doesn't stretch.

Fortunately, my husband thought differently. He reminded me to consider spiritual principles, not earthly fears and philosophies.

I grew up hearing phrases like "money doesn't grow on trees," "you have to work hard for money," and the biggest one, "we can't afford that!" Twenty-plus years of rigorous spiritual studies hadn't erased these old tapes playing in my head.

With more consideration, I saw where my thought process was off in the beginning, *teaching Mecca how far a dollar doesn't stretch*. As a divine being, why does she need to stretch a dollar?

Religious and spiritual texts teach about the abundant nature of the Universe. Over and over, I am called to remember that *abundance is our divine birthright*, that *the supply of the Universe is limitless,* and *I can be, do or have anything I can imagine and beyond*. There are countless expressions to lean on, but unless I'm actively practicing them, they are just words on a page.

Once at a spiritual meeting with our master teacher, a mother lamented about how stressed and disappointed she felt because she couldn't afford to buy her daughter all the things she wanted. The mother rambled on and on, not willing to hear any rebuttals to her circumstances. Finally, the spiritual master said something I will always remember: "Each child comes here with everything they need."

"But you don't understand, I can't afford to buy her..." the mother protested.

"Each child comes here with everything they need," the master reiterated. "You're only going to stop them from manifesting by thinking it's your responsibility to get everything for them."

Even though the mother couldn't hear this message, it was something that stuck deep inside of me. I have mentally referred back to that moment countless times when I worried about Mecca needing something I was afraid we couldn't afford. I stepped back, affirmed my daughter's divinity, and put the situation in the hands of her higher self. Over and over, miracles have occurred: I'd find the article at a crazy reduced price, someone would give it to her, or we'd receive the money to purchase it.

With all this said, we decided not to give Mecca an allowance. Instead, we talked to her about her ability to manifest whatever she needs from the quantum field. Our intention is for her to stay connected to her true source (God) and to call forth what she desires without the limitations of money.

There is definitely a challenge to this approach. She enjoys buying things with the money she receives as gifts and gets disappointed when she doesn't have enough to buy something. But we emphasize to her all of the things she has manifested without money like her first bike our neighbor gave her or the skateboard she found.

Most of her things come from me and my husband but I do feel we are on the right track. If someone had told me I was perfect and divine and talked to me about manifesting when I was a kid, I might have a different relationship with money today. We all have the opportunity to bring a new paradigm of prosperity to the next generation in spite of the beliefs we were raised with. Day by day I practice expanding my consciousness to embrace spiritual truths and turn away from worldly dogmas that teach a life of fear, struggle and sacrifice. For now, no allowance for Mecca.

BUT THE JACKETS ARE ON SALE

ven though we had lived in Atlanta for several years, I was still shocked by the chilly winters. A cold day in my hometown of Los Angeles was low to mid 50s. A wintry day in Atlanta was more like 20 degrees, and sometimes hit the mid-teens. So as a 'good' mother, of course I wanted my child to have ample warm clothing. Mecca had grown out of most of her wintertime gear and it was time to start anew.

First, I bought my daughter a beautiful purple, puffy, long coat, the kind with fake fur around the hood that mats the first time you wash it, to keep her snuggly during the frosty days. But since she's active and heats up quickly, the coat wasn't as practical as I wanted and certainly wasn't everyday wear.

"Hey Sweetie, Macy's has girls' jackets on sale!" I said excitedly after seeing a full-page ad in the paper.

"I don't need another jacket, I need boots," replied my 7-year-old.

"Well, let's go take a look. We haven't been to Lenox Square in a while. We can grab lunch and hang out."

"Okay, but you just bought me a coat last week and I want boots."

We lived in the suburbs and I loved driving into the city to shop at Lenox Square, a four-level upscale mall in the Buckhead district. The parkas were on sale for a killer price: regularly $80-$100 marked down to 20 bucks, what a deal!

The center was buzzing with shoppers as Mecca and I wove our way down the escalator to the crowded girls' section of the department store. Jackpot! Tons of adorable and functional jackets left in her size. I jumped right in.

"Oh, this one's cute," I held up a windbreaker for her to see.

"I don't really like it," she said with complete indifference.

"Why don't you look over on that rack, while I look through these?"

"Okay," she said and sauntered away.

When I looked for her to share what I found, she was in the toy section next to the girls' clothing, checking out various gadgets.

"How about these ski jackets? Do you like either one?"

She kind of turned up her nose while shaking her head and went back to perusing the playthings.

Not to be deterred from my mission, I rolled my eyes and returned to searching for a garment she would love. Ten minutes later I emerged triumphant with the perfect jackets: sleek, colorful, lightweight, yet warm. She had to be pleased with one of these.

I searched the area but couldn't find her. Once again, she was back in that darn toy section!

"Okay, what about these? Nice, aren't they? Why don't you try this one on?" I handed her a vibrant slicker.

She sighed as she laid down the gizmo to try on the covering.

"It fits perfectly! Turn to the mirror."

Her total lack of enthusiasm ultimately squashed my excitement. I felt irritation creeping up the back of my spine as if someone was scratching their fingernails across a blackboard.

"If you're not going to be helpful, we can just leave now!"

"Okay," she said.

Exasperated, I put down the jackets I was holding, hastily hung up the one she had tried on, and headed briskly to the escalator. *I'll show her,* I thought, hoping she would adjust her indifferent demeanor so that she could get new clothes.

She followed me, unaffected by my sudden and dramatic exit. As we rushed out of Macy's, a light bulb went off inside and I turned to my daughter.

"You told me at home you didn't want another jacket, didn't you?" finally grasping her disinterest in looking at coats.

"Yep! I need boots," she replied.

My bad…

I quickly dropped MY disagreeable attitude and went in search of boots for my daughter. Alas, I had wasted half an hour looking for unwanted outerwear, but oh well, such is life when I don't listen.

ICE BREAKERS:

Parents: Have you ever totally ignored what your child said they wanted and what happened?

Kids: Do your parents ever ignore your desires? If so, how does that make you feel?

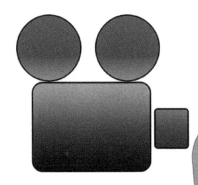

Strong-Willed Children!

Sandra, "If you are a parent and you think you have a strong-willed child, I can only suggest you look at yourself to see if you're trying to impose your position on your child to get them to comply to you instead of allowing your child to learn and grow and gain the inner strength that they may gain by making their own decisions, both good or bad, hurtful or powerful."

Link: https://youtu.be/zgSTbE0uQKk

SEX EDUCATION, YOU'RE NEVER TOO YOUNG OR TOO OLD

One thing I really love about Thomas' and my parenting style is that we seldom base things on what we did and didn't do as kids. We try to stay in the moment with Mecca and base our decisions on what's happening now. My daughter is far more evolved than I was at 6 years old, so it would be a disservice to her to live in my past.

With that said, I was in the local bookstore browsing and came across a book called *It's So Amazing! A Book about Eggs, Sperm, Birth, Babies and Families,* by Robie H. Harris and Michael Emberley. I looked through the volume and loved the clear, simple, and fun explanations, but thought Mecca was too young, so I put it back on the shelf. Have you ever felt drawn to something and can't walk away? I picked it up and put it back twice before finally purchasing it. Thomas was all for giving her the book and the reading began.

Mecca absolutely loved this book! Every time I turned around, she was reading it on her own, spelling out the words she didn't know, and it quickly became part of our nightly storytime. I think I bought the book to force me to deal with any discomfort I had about talking to her about sex, babies, the body, etc. The book was very clear, concise and detailed, yet was written for kids with funny pictures and characters which brought a lightness to the conversation.

What I was surprised by was her reaction to the content. She was totally fascinated that she was learning about the private parts of her body and men's bodies, but it was only information to her. She didn't have any of the baggage or judgments that I grew up with. I felt like I had truly opened the door to having open conversations with my daughter about absolutely anything and everything. Now that I had this book as a reference, my job was a lot easier. If I wasn't sure how to explain something to her in a way that was age appropriate, we could look for the answers together and both become more informed.

LET THE CHILDREN BE

ecently, I've had several conversations with parents who have pulled their children out of public school and are now homeschooling their kids. There are varying reasons, but the common denominator is dissatisfaction with the current system of education.

These past few years have ushered in a new energy of creativity, enlightenment, and connectedness with our higher selves. Our children are more advanced and aware than any generation before. They are demanding a new paradigm of education that supports who they are as spiritual beings and their life purpose. Anything else will be met with resistance or refusal to participate.

Unfortunately, many bright children in the school system are being mislabeled as difficult, slow or uncooperative. They are then disciplined for not fitting into a system that doesn't support them. They are made to feel wrong because of their behavior and too often medicated to try to control them.

I say, *Let our children be*! We each have a divine purpose to express, and maybe certain parts of traditional education don't support the purpose of many of our children. What if education actually focused on a child's interests and desires instead of passing tests?

We are moving into a higher level of consciousness as a society. We cannot expect to advance while clinging to old ways of being. Our children have come here with heightened awareness and solutions to age-old problems. Why don't we support them in their quests instead of hinder them with our outdated beliefs and fears?

My 6-year-old has been homeschooled from the start. She is an enthusiastic student (most of the time) who likes to stand on her head while we practice spelling. She is silly and smart and very independent and strong-willed. I think if she was forced to sit in a classroom for hours at a time, she would be labeled difficult because of her independence and spirited nature. A teacher with 30 students needs kids to conform, not express their individuality.

I understand homeschooling is not a viable option for everyone. It is a huge commitment many parents cannot make because of work and other obligations. And many children do thrive in school and are quite happy there. However, for those kids that just don't fit in, I ask parents to consider the change may need to occur in the school and not with your child. Maybe, just maybe your child is perfectly on track with their soul purpose which doesn't mesh with what and how they are being taught in school.

The energy and vibration of the future will not tolerate the status quo. Change is happening and education is a primary arena that needs to meet the current requirements of its students. Let the children be and redesign the institution.

8-11 YEARS

HOMESCHOOLING 301—MUCH MORE THAN LEARNING ONLINE

omeschooling involves considerably more than sitting at a computer studying. For the first few years of my daughter's education, Mecca and I would huddle together a couple of hours a day to complete her schoolwork. She liked all-inclusive workbooks like *Complete Curriculum* by Flash Kids Editors and *Brain Quest* by Various Authors. We'd study phonics, spelling and vocabulary, reading and writing, math, social studies, science and history. We'd usually go to the library to get away from household distractions and Mecca was an enthusiastic and attentive learner.

Around 10-years-old during her 5th grade year, my daughter became resistant and cranky whenever it was time to do coursework.

"Mecca, let's get ready to go to the library," I'd say, popping my head into her room.

"I don't feel like doing homework now."

"Well, it's getting late. When do you want to do it?"

"I don't know," her standard answer.

"Go ahead and get ready please."

Then when we arrived at the library, it took her forever to get her books out. She was lethargic and grumpy.

"What's going on?" I asked.

"I don't feel like doing homework. I'm tired." Sometimes she would even try to lay her head down on her folded arms.

"Well, it's study time. Pull it together," my frustration started to show.

I had always loved being my daughter's teacher. We had fun reviewing the lessons and talking through things. But I began dreading our schoolwork time. She wouldn't focus and barely participated—I felt myself nagging instead of encouraging her. Her education had deviated off course and I wasn't sure why or how. Something had to change, soon...

"What's up with you and homework?" I asked my daughter one day.

"Nothing."

"Every time we go to the library lately it's like pulling teeth to get you there, then you're always tired and kind of whiney."

"Sometimes I don't feel like studying when you want to," she said.

"Oh. Hmm." I thought for a moment. "What would work better for you then?"

"I don't know."

"I can't do anything with *I don't know*," I said. "Please think about it."

We regrouped later and came up with a brilliant solution that worked for both of us: we would continue to go to the library on Mondays, but instead of doing her assignments together, we would select lessons for her to complete throughout the week which would then be due on Fridays. She could study whenever she wanted as opposed to my prescribed times. On the following Monday we would review the prior week's work, then set up for the current week. It was great because it took the pressure off of both of us to fit into a schedule. Mecca had always been a night owl and she often worked on her assignments well into the evening. If she needed help with a task, we would work on it together (usually during the day when my mind was fresher).

Once we made this shift, my daughter's attitude improved immediately. She was once again the focused and enthusiastic student she had been. What I realized is that I hadn't been listening carefully to her. She had said numerous times that she didn't feel like studying 'now', not that she didn't 'want' to study. I was so focused on our schedule and the ways in which we'd done things in the past that I hadn't checked in with her to see if our process still worked for her.

With this change came added responsibility for Mecca. She would have to manage her time to finish her assignments by Fridays. The consequence if her lessons weren't done—no Netflix until completed. I began to view time management, self-regulation, self-motivation and communication as core instruction areas. These were skills I knew she would use for the rest of her life, and aptitudes I wished I had acquired at her age.

I've been very resourceful finding interesting and engaging ways for my child to acquire knowledge. One year I found this cool curriculum through Teachers Pay Teachers called *Travelling Through History With Doctor Who*, based around one of my daughter's favorite TV shows. *Doctor Who* is a British science fiction television program that portrays the escapades of a Time Lord called "The Doctor". We'd watch an episode together, then discuss the questions, and she'd pick an essay topic to answer. Granted, Queen Victoria didn't really fight werewolves nor did Winston Churchill defeat an evil race of alien robots that landed in London, still this curriculum broadened her awareness of historical events and figures in captivating ways. We spent countless hours conversing about significant turning points in the world, what worked and didn't work in her essays, and the various exploits of the Doctor.

Another year, I used a MasterClass entitled *Scientific Thinking and Communication* taught by astrophysicist Neil deGrasse Tyson to incorporate the theories we had studied in our astronomy co-op with critical, real-world thinking skills. MasterClass is an immersive online experience taught by masters in a particular field of study and Dr. Tyson is particularly interesting and entertaining. A powerful concept from this class we repeatedly used is what Dr. Tyson called "informed skepticism—the ability to ask the right questions—which keeps us from being manipulated." This concept applied not only to her studies either. If Thomas or I, but mostly Thomas, said something that didn't sound right to her she definitely called us out on it. She'd start by saying something like, "That doesn't make sense," then launch into her reasoning.

Additionally, Mecca has been doing monthly and year-end presentations almost since the beginning. For her monthly talks, she could pick any topic she wanted. The point was to discover how to research, organize and communicate her thoughts more so than any specific subject matter. Oftentimes she did PowerPoint Presentations, but she also created models and display boards. It was awesome watching her confidence grow—she began standing up straight, holding her head high, projecting her voice, and making eye contact while explaining her assignments, instead of just reading off her notes like a routine grocery list. To finalize the end of each grade, she would do a year-end presentation summarizing the workbooks, classes and activities she had participated in for the two semesters.

Throughout the years, we've had several hits and misses when it comes to projects and presentations. A few of my favorites were a board game made up of planets in our solar system, and two historical fiction stories—one about women getting the right to vote and the other about Adolf Hitler. A couple of the standout misses were an ill-conceived puppet show that kept collapsing during her demonstration, and an ineffective comparison of disasters. A bit more about that one...

For an 8th grade project, Mecca wanted to do a series of three presentations to determine what type of disaster would wipe out humanity the fastest between a cosmic, man-made or natural disaster. Her cosmic disaster (an asteroid) and man-made disaster (nuclear war) facts were pretty convincing, but she came up short on her natural disaster evidence.

"Hmm, so you think an earthquake on the Cascadia Subduction Zone on the west coast of the U.S. would wipe out humanity?" I asked toward the end of her questionable exhibition.

"Yeah. Maybe?"

"Really? I don't think so given the evidence you've presented. What do you think, Thomas?"

"I don't think so either," he said.

"Okay, let me ask you this." I said to Mecca. "How long did you have to do this assignment?"

"A month."

"And when did you start working on it?"

"A couple of days ago," she answered sheepishly.

"And when did you discover that your theory didn't hold up?"

"Last night," she laughed because she knew where I was heading with my questioning.

"So. You waited until the last minute again?"

"Well, I thought I would have plenty of time, but when I realized an earthquake wouldn't wipe out humanity quickly, I didn't have time to change it," she explained.

"Okay, so even you knew your theory didn't hold up before you started this presentation?" I asked.

"Yep!"

"Did you think we wouldn't notice?"

"I gave it about a 50/50 chance," she said smugly.

I rolled my eyes. "Redo your presentation. And how about putting a little more effort into it. This is your education, you know."

"Okay."

"The presentations are as much about managing your time as well as the research and communication," I said.

"I know, I know," she said as she scurried out our bedroom door. She'd heard it all before and yet she still waited until the last minute.

The following month, her super volcano theory was better researched and more convincing. I'm sure she didn't spend more than a few days working on it, but at least it wasn't slapped together like her earthquake address. Her conclusion was an asteroid would kill off humanity the fastest out of the three events. Every monthly demonstration provided opportunities for growth and development, both in the subject matter studied and in the process of presenting or even revising a talk.

❄ ❄ ❄

The COVID-19 global pandemic hit the United States in March 2020, toward the end of Mecca's 8th grade year. Parents, teachers and students scrambled to figure out how to continue their education. 'Homeschooling' became the norm since schools were closed and it was not possible to meet in person.

As a full-time, long-term homeschool parent, I didn't consider this trend of taking classes online homeschooling. Simply taking a public or private school curriculum and moving it to a virtual portal does not constitute homeschooling to me and the other homeschool families I've talked with. For us, choosing to homeschool our children was a conscious, deliberate choice. It was a lifestyle choice. It was not done by default or because of a global pandemic. There are as many ways to homeschool as there are families. From what I've seen each family has its own method, their own process based on their values and priorities. I like to think of my daughter's education as concierge instruction; it is specifically tailored to her needs and interests, her particular learning style and schedule. I've spent incalculable hours planning her education and activities. I've spent hundreds of hours finding and attending homeschool days at art and natural history museums, aquariums, science centers, children's museums, botanical gardens, zoos, nature centers, planetariums, children's theatres, concerts and puppet shows, and nature walks. You name it, we've probably done it. In addition, unlike a public school where books and supplies are provided, homeschoolers are responsible for purchasing (or bartering) ALL the books, supplies, classes and lessons our kids take. We pay taxes to support our local school system, but we also pay to educate our children in both time and money.

So, you see, homeschooling a child involves much more than just learning online; it is an intentional choice made by millions of families who do it willingly and lovingly. From my perspective, it is one of the biggest commitments I've ever made, and requires patience, diligence, creativity, spontaneity and flexibility. It is not a static process but an ever-evolving practice—it changes as my child grows and develops. When it doesn't shift, or if I'm not willing to make simple adjustments like with our school work schedule, my child could quickly turn from a self-motivated pupil into a disgruntled automaton, going through the motions of learning, but not actually acquiring any knowledge. Happily, it has worked well for us and is worth every dollar, minute, hour, day and year we've invested in it.

WHAT DOES A MOLE ON MY HUSBAND'S FACE HAVE TO DO WITH MY DAUGHTER'S STOMACH ACHE?

ne day, my very healthy and fit 8-year-old daughter began having recurrent stomach aches. Foods she had eaten for years upset her stomach after one small bite. She was sluggish and whiny and had a hard time getting through a meal.

I became so concerned I briefly considered taking her to an allopathic doctor, something we rarely do; we prefer homeopathic remedies. But instead, I turned back to our spiritual principles to look at what was going on in my household that could be upsetting her. According to Louise Hay's book, *Heal Your Body, The Mental Causes For Physical Illness and the Metaphysical Way To Overcome Them*, stomach and intestinal problems have to do with dread, fear of the new or not feeling nourished (Hay 66). Well, it wasn't too difficult to identify the issue.

Six months prior, a small dark spot appeared suddenly on the right side of my husband's face about an inch from his nose. He had lots of moles and freckles so at first it was no big deal. We kept watching the spot for changes and noticed that it was odd looking, not smooth like his other marks, but kind of flakey. After a month, I started insisting he get it checked out by a dermatologist. It took him a while before he finally set up an appointment. The doctor recommended he have the mole biopsied. He immediately went in for another opinion; the second doctor had the same advice. This was about the time my stomach tightened with a sense of dread. Thomas was nervous as well but he put on a brave face. We told Mecca the reason for my hubby's sudden and repeated visits to the doctor. We thought we were keeping it light so she wouldn't worry.

The closer we got to my husband's biopsy date, the more frequent were her tummy aches. Even though our explanations were lighthearted, she picked up on our fear energy, which then outpictured as her stomach aches. I worked with her on deep breathing and grounding techniques which helped quite a bit, all the time recognizing that as long as we were afraid, she would be also, even if she never said a word about it.

The biopsy confirmed our worst fears, the mole was melanoma skin cancer, the most serious and aggressive type. It can spread to other parts of the body and get in the lymph nodes.

My heart sank, my stomach hurt and it was difficult for me to stay grounded for a few days. My dad had passed away from cancer a couple of months before and my mind kept drifting in fear of losing my husband to this disease as well. I finally pulled myself together and realized that Thomas was not ailing like my father had and his diagnosis was very different.

Once Thomas had his outpatient surgery and we got the all clear that he was cancer free, his energy shifted immediately—calmer and more peaceful, as did mine. My insides felt settled for the first time in weeks.

Shortly after receiving the good news, Mecca's stomach aches completely disappeared. She ate most of the food on her plate and didn't once cry out, "Mommy my tummy hurts," in that sad voice with teary eyes. She returned to being the happy and carefree child that we knew her to be.

Bottom line, her stomach aches were simply mirroring back to us our fear and dread about Thomas' skin cancer diagnosis, and weren't an illness or virus on her part. I'm glad we worked that out before making an unnecessary trip to the doctor.

ICE BREAKERS:

Parents: Have you ever noticed your kids get sick when there's stress in your household?

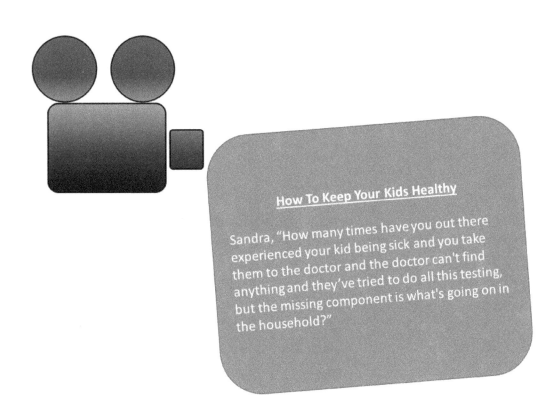

How To Keep Your Kids Healthy

Sandra, "How many times have you out there experienced your kid being sick and you take them to the doctor and the doctor can't find anything and they've tried to do all this testing, but the missing component is what's going on in the household?"

Link: https://youtu.be/zmgT5uiDEpY

HE GOT 2 PRESENTS, I GOT NADA

I love Christmas! When I was a kid, I'd start counting down the days until the 25th on December 1st. I couldn't wait to ride my sleek new bike or play with the beautiful doll I had wanted all year. As a mom, I basked in watching my 8-year-old daughter's face brighten as she ripped the wrapping paper off her presents, or proudly passed a gift she'd made for me.

On this sunny Christmas morning, Mecca opened her first present, then Thomas opened one from her, and I opened one from Thomas. I took pictures and relished the scene. Then, Mecca gave Thomas a second present. I waited expectantly for my artsy gift from her as the presents cleared from under the tree.

She finally said, "That's it!"

My eyes widened—no more presents? Confusion set in. *Where's my present from Mecca?* I wondered.

I looked on as they laughed and reveled in their gifts. I even smiled a bit though my heart was aching. I finally went to the bathroom so they wouldn't see me cry.

My sadness and disappointment turned into anger. I glared in the mirror and snapped, *What the f! I'm the one who takes her to 90% of her activities. I'm the one who makes her dinner, homeschools her and tucks her in at night, and he gets two presents and I get NOTHING!!"*

This diatribe in my mind went on for another minute or so. *How inconsiderate, ungrateful and mean… Wait a minute, Mecca's not any of those things.*

I caught my breath. *If Mecca is usually very generous and loving, what happened that she didn't make me a present?* I asked myself.

I washed my face, decided not to question my daughter about my lack of a gift until I received clarity, and returned to the living room to be with my family. I put my distress in a box so that I wouldn't ruin the day for them.

Two or three days later I had an 'aha' moment that shook me: in May, Mecca had given me a Mother's Day present with a cute little stuffed animal attached to it. One day I was decluttering and gave the animal back to her because I didn't want it to go to waste. When I handed it to her, she gave me a weird look, but took it without saying anything.

Okay, it was time to talk to her. I went to her bedroom and found her on the floor playing with her Legos.

"Honey, I noticed you didn't make me a present for Christmas. Can I ask why?"

"I don't know," her stock answer to everything.

"Well, I've been thinking about it. Is it because I gave part of your Mother's Day present back to you?"

"Yes," she answered in a small voice.

"Did you feel like I didn't value what you had given me?"

"Yes." Her eyes watered so I knew I had nailed it!

"Come here, I want to show you something."

She followed me into my bedroom. I opened a drawer and pulled out a manila envelope marked 'Mementos from Mecca' and showed her a stack of cards and trinkets that I had amassed over the years.

"Honey, I'm so sorry I returned your gift. I want you to know that I love and value all the things you've made for me. See all of this stuff I've saved?"

She nodded yes.

"Mommy had a brain fart. I thought I was being considerate, but I see now how that would make you feel like I didn't care about the things you have given me."

I hugged her. She loosely hugged me back.

"Will you forgive me?"

She slowly nodded yes. We sat for a moment and loved each other.

"Is there anything you'd like to say about it?" I asked.

"No."

I gave her a kiss and she scrambled away from me, relieved that conversation was over. I hoped that I had resolved the conflict, but since she hadn't said much, it was difficult to tell.

A couple of months later she made me a lovely Valentine's Day present.

"Thank you Honey." I hugged her tightly. My eyes teared with appreciation that she had forgiven me.

I ACCUSED HER OF BEING UNPREPARED

y 9-year-old daughter was so excited to attend her Girl Scouts roller skating party—five hours of loud music, pizza and fun with her friends! I was excited to have a five-hour date with my husband with no babysitter to pay. A good day was in store for all.

As we walked out of the house, I asked Mecca if she had everything she needed and reminded her that we weren't staying for the event. She said yes, and we left.

So how did Thomas and I turn a celebratory party into unnecessary chaos? One step at a time.

Mecca arrived at the rink with her socks, water bottle and protein bar fully ready to skate. At the last minute, I decided to give her money in case she wanted to buy something. Five hours seemed like a long time to leave her without any resources.

"Do you have pockets or a backpack to put the money in?" I asked as I handed her a $10 bill.

"No," she answered simply. I immediately got annoyed.

"Why don't you have a bag? Where are you going to put the money?

"You didn't tell me to bring a bag. I don't know."

That's when I started my diatribe about her not being prepared. "You don't have a place to put ANYTHING! Money, jacket, snacks."

She just stood there waiting for me to finish. She had nothing else to say about it.

A couple of minutes later, Thomas joined us and asked if I had the troop leader's cell phone number so we could leave and catch our movie in time.

"No, she doesn't have a cell phone," I said.

"I'm not leaving my daughter for five hours without a phone," he declared. He turned to Mecca who was looking longingly at the giggling skaters and had already tuned us out.

"Mecca, where's your cell phone?"

"It's in the car."

"Why is it in the car?"

"I didn't bring it in."

"Why don't you have your phone with you?"

"I don't know," she said with a blank stare.

"I haven't bought minutes for her phone in at least three months, so she doesn't have cell service anyway." I told him. "And, I'm not leaving my phone with her because she has no place to put it."

He lectured her as well about not having a bag for her stuff, then spent 20 minutes on the phone with our carrier to reactivate Mecca's service.

At this point, 30 minutes of our precious date time had wasted away. While Thomas and I worked things out, Mecca scurried away to put her skates on.

My husband finally completed the lengthy transaction with the phone company, and we thought all was well until I called the number to make sure it was working and some random guy answered. Turned out they had given my daughter's number away for non-usage. Thomas had added minutes to someone else's phone!

The clock ticked on. We had been dashing around the roller rink for 45 minutes instead of romancing on our prearranged date.

Fed up, I found the co-leader of Mecca's troop—she indeed had a cell phone. We exchanged numbers, my hubby and I kissed Mecca goodbye and left.

I wasn't sure our date could be salvaged since we were both grumpy and irritated...

We grabbed lunch at a grocery store deli before heading to the movies. We sat at a small table near the front by the windows and unwound.

"You know, I thought about what happened at the rink, and maybe it wasn't really Mecca's fault," I said out of the blue.

"What do you mean?"

"Well, she didn't ask me for money, I wanted her to have it. Then I got mad at her because she didn't have anywhere to put it. And she didn't ask for a phone, you insisted she have one."

Thomas nodded thoughtfully. We ate and talked. We wanted to clear the air so we could actually enjoy our valued date time.

"Yeah, I was a bit hard on her," Thomas admitted with regret.

"Me too," I said. "You know, we both accused her of being unprepared, but really she had what she wanted and needed: her socks, water, and a protein bar for her snack."

"And she knew they were serving pizza, so lunch was covered," Thomas added.

"Actually, she hadn't asked for anything."

"I think we may have projected our needs onto her."

"Then we made her wrong for not living up to our expectations," I said.

"We should probably apologize to her," he said.

"Yep!" We stared out the window.

"Can we have some fun now that we've worked that out?" Thomas asked.

"Oh yeah!" I said.

* * *

When we picked Mecca up later that afternoon, we apologized for making her wrong, and explained our epiphanies about projecting our needs onto her. We thought she'd be grateful and gracious, but she wasn't.

"Hmph, I know. I brought what I needed and wanted." Thomas and I rolled our eyes at each other and finally laughed about the whole incident.

After this experience, I shifted my approach to preparing to leave the house. I would ask my daughter if she had what she needed instead of listing a bunch of items I thought were necessary, like I used to. This allowed her to be more responsible and took the pressure off me to handle everything. I also became less accommodating (and frustrated) when she forgot to bring a sweater and was cold, or she forgot her book and said 'I'm bored' from the back seat of the car. I stopped jumping to immediately fix everything for her.

By the way, she bought 60 tokens with the $10 I gave her and played arcade games with her friends. She was the hit of the party!

I ACCUSED HER OF BEING UNPREPARED, PART 2

WRITTEN BY MECCA JONES-KELLER

henever my parents dropped me off somewhere, I always made sure I had everything I needed no matter where I was going, and it was no different when I was preparing to go to my Girl Scouts roller-skating event. I had brought exactly what I deemed as the essentials to have a good time at the rink: some water, a snack to hold me until we had pizza, and socks for the skates. If it turned out I needed or wanted something else, then I would just have to deal with it and make do with what I did have.

I was confident and perfectly happy with what I had brought, so you can imagine my annoyance when my parents started going into an unnecessary panic about my "lack of things I needed to be prepared". I leaned against the wall and longingly stared out at my troop (who for some reason didn't sell cookies) having fun skating and dancing to music. All I wanted was to join them, but I was held back by my mom lecturing me while my dad stood outside trying to reach the phone company to get my phone working. My parents were in a frenzy about something that I had under control.

Eventually, after at least 45 minutes and quite a bit of wasted skating time, my parents were finally at peace when they found out the assistant troop leader did have a phone. Now, they had a way to contact me since mine wasn't working and finally left to go on their date. I was happy to be free and excitedly began skating, desperately wanting to make up for lost time with friends.

Luckily, an experience like that hasn't happened again since my parents are more aware that their teachings of self-responsibility were successfully taught to me. Occasionally, they will double check to make sure I have everything I need, to which I just nod my head because I have already prepared for wherever I'm going and know how to take care of myself.

MY DAUGHTER WAS SO MAD SHE MADE HERSELF SICK

was having a peaceful morning until my 9-year-old daughter dragged herself into my room and whined, "Mommy, my head and stomach hurt." I was in the middle of something so had to switch gears quickly. I thought for a moment before I answered her.

"Hmm," I said. "You were pretty mad all afternoon yesterday. Ask your body if that's why you don't feel well today."

She took a deep breath, closed her eyes and went within for a moment. She opened her tear-filled eyes and nodded yes.

"Now ask your body what it needs to release this negative energy that's making you feel so bad."

"A warm bath," she moaned.

I finished what I was doing and ran a soothing bath for her. The day before she was mad because she had to leave a homeschool art event that my husband had taken her to at our local museum much earlier than she had expected. When I've taken her to activities, I usually allow her to stay as long as she wants, but my husband wasn't as patient on this day.

It was unusual for Mecca to remain upset for so long. One of the things I admired about her was her ability to process feelings and move on—she was typically back to her cheerful self within minutes. This time, however, she was grumpy for half the day. She even had to take a nap because she tired herself out with her bad mood, and was still cranky when she woke up.

We've discussed Universal Laws with my daughter for years and relish opportunities to bring them into a conversation. In our spiritual study group, one of our primary texts was *The Kybalion: A Study of the Hermetic Philosophy of Ancient Egypt and Greece*, by the Three Initiates, which outlined seven principles that govern the Universe. Two of those principles which resonated in this moment were the Laws of Mentalism and Vibration.

First, we talked about how everything started with her thoughts: she was mad about leaving the museum early, was mad at her dad, and was testy all afternoon. All her negative thoughts hurt her body and manifested as a headache and stomach ache. Because this happened so quickly, we were able to link it together. Had she gotten sick a few days later, we probably would have forgotten about her getting angry, which lowered her vibration and caused the aches and pains. We may have attributed her discomfort to a 'bug', and missed the whole lesson entirely.

I find these teaching moments move us all forward in our spiritual evolution. *This was a great reminder that I cannot have sick thoughts (anger) and maintain a healthy body.* My prolonged anger and frustration toward anybody only hurts myself. I saw this clearly with Mecca and hope to remember it the next time I get upset. I'm not saying that one shouldn't get mad. But what I have a tendency to do is to hold onto the anger far longer than warranted. In Mecca's case, she had fully expressed herself about her disappointment and dismay, we had acknowledged her, but then she continued to be aggravated for hours. I believe that's what finally hurt her body, seething in the distress.

I wish I had learned these lessons when I was a kid—it would have saved me years of suffering. My intention is for Mecca to own her power in creating all of her life, the good and the unpleasant. I feel that the more she learns this now, the clearer (and happier) she will be!

ICE BREAKERS:

Kids: Have you ever gotten so mad you made yourself sick? If so, how?

IS THIS SHIRT CLEAN OR DIRTY?

never minded doing laundry. I had set aside a couple of mornings a week when I knew we'd be home to get the housework done. Mecca slept in while I completed my tasks.

This worked for years until...

"Ouch!" I yelped as I stepped on a Lego hidden beneath a dirty shirt.

"What are you doing?" my groggy 9-year-old asked as she lifted her head from underneath the dozen stuffed animals surrounding her pillow.

"Trying to figure out which clothes are dirty so I can do laundry," I said, picking through tops, jeans and underwear scattered across the floor.

"Oh." She adjusted her position and went back to sleep.

Why can't this child put dirty clothes in the basket and clean clothes in the drawers like I've asked her? I muttered to myself for the millionth time. Impatiently, I threw all of her clothes in my basket instead of sorting through them, wasting both my time and water by laundering already clean clothes.

After I washed and folded her clothes, I placed the neat pile back in her room for her to put away. Several days later the clean folded outfits had mixed with the dirty apparel on the floor.

"Hey Honey, why are those clean clothes on the floor?"

"Because I haven't put them away yet," she answered. I sighed and walked away.

On this particular morning, I walked into Mecca's dimly lit room and gasped at the usual disarray on her floor: shorts and tops piled in small clusters, various Lego models under construction, arts and craft supplies cluttered into corners, and shoes, workbooks, and stuffed animals layered on the floor, so that only patches of carpet were visible.

I'm not looking through this crap for dirty clothes, I mumbled to myself as I quietly backed out of her room, not wanting to wake her.

A couple of hours later, Mecca called out, "Mom, did you wash my black leggings?" while she scrambled for something clean to put on.

"Nope! Honey, I think at 9, you're old enough to do your own laundry," I said calmly.

"Huh?" she said.

"Yep! I'm tired of digging through your room to figure out what's clean and what's dirty. I'm done asking you to put away the clothes I've spent my time washing and folding. And I'm fed up with poking my feet on Legos trying to gather your clothes."

"Oh," she said and seemed to contemplate.

"I'll show you how to do your laundry, and I'll help you, but I'm not going to sort through that crap on your floor anymore to get to it," I explained.

Over the following weeks, I taught my daughter how to wash and dry her clothes. Even though I showed her how to sort them, she preferred to lump all her garments into one large load after she ran out of things to wear.

Additionally, since her laundry was her responsibility, I kept my mouth shut about when she did it. Quite often I heard the washing machine start after midnight, which meant her clothes wouldn't be put into the dryer until morning when we were preparing to leave the house. I've learned that just because I hated wearing damp clothes, she did not.

MY DAUGHTER IS SO BUSTED!

ne night my 8-year-old daughter was watching Netflix in her room and jumped as I entered. When I looked at the computer screen it was on the home page. I asked her what she was watching and she said *My Little Pony*. She was acting weird and a little too eager to get rid of me so I opened the Netflix page and *The Suite Life of Zack and Cody* came up.

"What's that?" I asked.

"I don't know what that show is. Can you put it back on *My Little Pony*? she said, trying to act innocent.

I knew she was lying, but left her room without making a big deal out of it. I wanted to contemplate why she would fib to watch a children's show. Even as I turned to leave, I felt pulled to stay and lecture her, however, a wiser part knew to look at mirroring first.

Thomas and I use mirroring as one of our main parenting tools. What is mirroring, you may wonder? In a nutshell mirroring means: 'If you see it, you be it'. In other words, the person in front of me is mirroring back (showing me) something I'm either thinking or doing. Basically, they are showing me myself.

Yuck! Sometimes I really hate mirroring. I didn't like what I was seeing in my daughter at that moment and certainly didn't want to look at that part of *yours truly*. I liked to think of myself as powerful, honest and certain. Well, Mecca's energy was timid, weird and secretive.

I set the intention for clarity and guidance before going to bed. By morning, during meditation, things became crystal clear.

A few hours prior to the incident with Mecca, I had offered to give a close friend a promotion code to a professional membership website I was involved in that would give her free access for a month. As soon as I made the offer, I questioned my integrity. As far as I knew, the promotion code was to be used only during our soft launch, which was a month before. To justify my actions, I made excuses in my mind for giving her the code, trying to minimize the guilt that I felt. Bottom line, I felt weird and secretive, the exact same things I had seen in Mecca.

To remedy the situation, I asked the organizers if it was okay that I gave out the code. I received a big *yes*! I was relieved that I no longer had to hide or make excuses and went to talk to my daughter.

Our conversation was pretty brief, like most of them are, since I'm the one doing a majority of the talking. I found her relaxing in her room and sat down next to her.

"Sweetie, I want you to be powerful in your life. I felt like you were being really weird and weak when I asked you about *The Suite Life of Zack and Cody*. Is there any reason why you shouldn't watch that show?" I asked.

"I don't know," she said.

I expected her response after years of hearing *I don't knows* whenever she didn't want to consider an answer.

"Can you think about it for a minute," I said and waited patiently. She fidgeted. "What was going through your mind?"

"I wasn't sure about watching the show because you weren't familiar with it," she finally said.

"Hmm. That makes sense. What is the show about?"

"It's a kids show about two twin brothers who live in a hotel with their mom."

"That sounds okay. Can I see a clip?" Mecca hit play and we watched a few minutes of the silly comedy.

"I think that's just fine for you to watch. Okay?"

"Okay," she said.

We talked about mirroring and I explained how I felt out of integrity and weird when I offered my friend the free promotion code.

"Yeah, I was wondering about that when you were talking to her," she said. My daughter had questioned my actions as well.

"Oh, I didn't know you had heard me."

"Yep!"

"How about this," I said. "If you're not sure about something, just ask. It's better to get clarity than hide out feeling you've done something wrong. Agreed?"

"Okay," she said.

Oftentimes I've found in my life that my big declarations initially have the opposite effect of what I've intended. In this case, I had committed to being clear and powerful as a member of this professional website, only to undermine myself when I gave a friend free access. Thanks to my daughter's secretive behavior and mirroring, I confronted my own lack of integrity and asked about the promotion code instead of wallowing in guilt. The more I clean up my own mess, the more peaceful my child can be. It would have been hypocritical to lecture Mecca, when I had done something similar just hours before.

Are You Terrified Your Kids Are Going To Be Like You Were?

Thomas, "...It caught me very emotionally because I have a 12-year-old daughter now and I was thinking back to my teens and the struggles that I went through finding and searching for peace...and what I realized was I didn't want my daughter to have to go through the struggles that I went through because I knew how painful that had been for myself and the people around me."

Link: https://youtu.be/EJJuYO5pm6A

THAT CYST ISN'T GOING AWAY

hen I first noticed a small bump on my 10-year-old daughter's neck, I thought it was a bug bite. It was a circular raised dot, not red or irritated, just sitting there. Then I observed the bump was still there a couple of weeks later.

"Sweetie, I see you still have that bump on your neck. Do you remember getting bit by a bug or something?" I asked.

"I don't know."

"Well, how long has it been there?"

"I don't remember."

"Is it bothering you? Does it itch or anything?"

"No."

"Hmm, okay, let's keep an eye on it."

"Okay," she said as she walked away, hoping I would just drop it.

The next time I inspected the bump, it appeared to be a solid knot rather than a bug bite. Had it been on her finger, I would have thought she had a splinter; however, given the location, it couldn't be. It was time to examine the lump a bit closer—I found the brightest lamp in our house and lugged it into the bathroom.

"Let's take a look at your bump under the light," I said.

"Okay, but it's fine," she mumbled.

I put on my glasses to take a closer look. A greenish lump had formed under the skin.

"Hey Thomas, can you come look at Mecca's neck?" I called out. We both examined her neck under the spotlight while she sighed heavily and insisted it was okay.

"I can't tell what it is," he said. "Does it hurt?" he asked her.

"No."

"What do you think it needs to heal itself?" I asked, wanting her to participate.

She closed her eyes, became still and quiet, while she mentally scanned her neck and checked in with her body like I've taught her to do whenever something is going on.

"It will be fine," she announced.

"Well, why don't we put a hot compress on it to break up whatever is in there?" I suggested.

"Okay," she agreed reluctantly.

We placed multiple compresses on her neck over the next few days. Finally, a whitish head formed on it that looked like a pimple ready to burst. I thought it would extract easily, but it didn't. A bit of pus oozed out, however, a solid object remained buried in her skin.

Several days later, we all gathered in the bathroom again and assessed the progress. The bump was still there.

"Maybe we should take you to a doctor," Thomas suggested.

"No! It will be fine," Mecca said.

"Well, what are you going to do about it? This has been going on for a while now," I said.

"I'll do energy work on it, just leave it alone," she told us. "I said it will be fine."

Energy work involves tapping into the body's own frequencies to remove blocks and gather information and direction, ultimately so the body's innate intelligence can heal itself. I've been doing energy work with and on Mecca since before she was born, teaching her to be in tune with her body and empowering her to trust her intuition. I didn't want my concerns to undermine her confidence in communicating with her body, yet I didn't want this bump to turn into something serious.

After checking in with my intuition, I decided to trust her.

"Okay, since it's not bothering her, let's give it a few more days," I said to both of them.

Over the course of several weeks, the bump went through various incarnations: it got pussy, popped, oozed, and split open before finally pushing out a hard, black ant-sized core, and then healing itself. At one point it was so gross I insisted Mecca wear a scarf to cover it up.

Through all of this, Mecca remained confident in her ability to heal her neck. It was really quite amazing to watch. Her confidence never wavered and she knew that she could dissolve the cyst (or whatever it was.) Now, if I'm concerned about something going on with her and she's not, she'll remind me, "I healed my neck!" with great pride, pretty much telling me to leave her alone.

THAT CYST ISN'T GOING AWAY, PART 2

WRITTEN BY MECCA JONES-KELLER

have had many minor injuries, infections, and bug bites during my life that have healed on their own, so when I first noticed the weird bump on my neck, I wasn't very concerned.

My mom is an energy healer, and for as long as I can remember I've been taught how to internally assess any issues that may arise concerning my body, and ask it what it needs to heal itself. At first, I would have to close my eyes, tune in, and wait to hear an answer in my mind, but after doing this for so many years, I'm able to determine the severity of something in just a few seconds without having to close my eyes and tune in. It just will come to me and then I can provide it with whatever solution it needs. So, that's exactly what I did with the bump on my neck.

In the beginning, I thought it was some sort of bug bite, but as the weeks progressed, it grew bigger and occasionally produced pus. During each phase of its progression, I made sure to check in to see if it needed anything to help it heal. Every time I did, I was assured that it was harmless and would heal In Its own time without the need of any outside help such as a doctor. I was confident in my body and intuition, so I was never very concerned or scared about the bump. I knew it would be fine and take care of itself.

Eventually, as it got grosser and filled with more pus, my mom insisted I wear a scarf to cover the disgusting (now thought to be) cyst, displayed on my neck.

One day, after weeks of building up, the cyst popped when I came out of a hot shower. I made sure to squeeze any excess pus out, and along with it came a small, hard black ball. After the lump finally popped, my neck quickly healed and would have been restored back to its normal look if I hadn't accidentally scratched it when it was itchy, making it leave a tiny scar.

To this day, I still don't know exactly how or why I had a cyst of sorts on my neck, or what the small black ball was that came out. But I do trust my intuition, and as long as I know that whatever is going on is harmless and doesn't bother me, it will all be okay. Eventually it will heal, even if it might need a little help.

12-15 YEARS

HOMESCHOOLING 401—TRANSITIONING TO HIGH SCHOOL

nce we started homeschooling, the thought was to continue to do it as long as it worked for all of us. It wasn't necessarily a 13-year commitment carved in stone. Every couple of years we'd reevaluate to determine if we were going to continue. Each time was a resounding *Yes*! Mecca continued to thrive, I enjoyed teaching and learning with her, and Thomas loved the fact that we guided her education.

In Mecca's 8th grade year, I asked her if she wanted to go to a public high school. She quickly said no, but I requested that she think about it. There were several things I had really enjoyed about high school like cheerleading, Friday night football games, learning with fellow students, parties and dances. I didn't want her to miss out on any part of the huge social aspects of school.

A couple of weeks later she stated very clearly, "I have no desire to go to high school next year."

"Why not?" I asked.

"I don't want to wake up early. I don't want to have to spend the whole day in school. I don't want to have that much homework, and I don't want to be around that many people all day."

All I could say was, "Okay."

I was apprehensive about high school. I didn't know about transcripts or course and graduation requirements. Mecca said she wanted to go to college, which meant she'd have to meet certain prerequisites. From that point on I started thinking about a comprehensive high school curriculum. For me this was serious go-time! Up until then, my daughter had used workbooks (lots of *Brain-Quest*), taken courses on both Outschool and Khan Academy (online learning platforms), participated in a weekly science cooperative with other homeschool families, and anything else I could piece together to support her interests and educational needs. We reviewed and discussed her school work, but I never really graded her. I figured no one cared about her primary and middle school scores, and I had an internal grading system that I used to measure her progress: could she communicate what she learned clearly and effectively while applying critical thinking skills? Could she make connections between the past and the present? I didn't care so much about dates, but big picture stuff. Could she organize her projects and manage her schedule to complete her school work and ice skate three times a week?

My internal system had guided me successfully for years, but I felt differently about high school. This was unchartered territory that would be a precursor to her future—her chances of scholarships and school choices. People cared about her high school marks. College admission counselors would scrutinize her based on her test scores and grades from now on. In the past, when I would question if I was doing a good job with my daughter's education, she would end up saying or doing something to affirm that she was on the right track. This type of confirmation wasn't going to be enough anymore.

Once I set the intention to prepare for high school, everything I needed fell into place. On a conference call with our co-op moms, one of the mothers mentioned that Florida Virtual School (FLVS, the first statewide internet-based public high school in the United States) has guidance counselors to consult with, and someone else shared resources about transcripts and record keeping.

Mecca and I spent an hour on the phone with a guidance counselor as she walked us through planning for high school. I had a long list of questions which she patiently answered one by one. By the end of the call, I knew what classes were required, how many units were needed to graduate, how to track the units, how many volunteer hours were required for state sponsored scholarships, how to document transcripts and how to get a notarized document of graduation which is what she'll receive instead of a diploma. Whew! The counselor emailed me sample forms and resources to support me. I jumped into action—I designed a form to log her volunteer hours and created a blank transcript to keep track of her classes as we went along instead of trying to gather everything in her senior year. I felt ready, not scared and unsure of myself anymore.

Mecca enrolled in the FLVS Flex Program for high school which meant she could pick and choose what classes she took and when she would take them. She could set her own pace, and the teachers hold daily office hours between 8am and 8pm and send out regular updates. We could call, text or email them with any questions or concerns. Mecca took FLVS Language Arts in 8th grade and liked it. It was well organized, comprehensive, and easy to understand, which led us to sign up for FLVS high school courses. After all the years of working primarily with me, she liked receiving grades and having definitive deadlines for her assignments. Fortunately, she is self-motivated and developed good study and time management skills required to work independently online.

Unfortunately, after years of meeting in person, our weekly family co-op had to shift to online due to the COVID-19 pandemic. These gatherings were Mecca's opportunity to learn and socialize with her friends. They would break into groups fostering teamwork and collaboration, chat during snack time, and hang out for a bit afterwards. Every now and then I would check in with her about it.

"How do you like meeting online for co-op?" I asked.

"I liked it better in person. I miss seeing my friends."

"Yeah, me too."

"But I don't have to wake up early to get ready to go in person," she added. I guess there's a bright spot to everything.

My role as homeschool educator has changed significantly. I no longer have to come up with my child's curriculum or evaluate her work. I'm more of a supervisor now. I talk to her teachers, ask questions, act as go-between, give general feedback on assignments when asked, and make sure she's getting what she needs overall. And I'll assist her with homework when needed. I helped her with Algebra 1 until it became apparent that she needed to work with someone who understood the complexities of it better than I did. It was a big moment for me to realize she needed more than I could give her, since I'd been her primary teacher for all of her education. We found an excellent tutor who simplified the complex problems in a way that Mecca easily understood. My daughter relaxed, and I relaxed knowing that we finally had proper support for math.

At the end of Mecca's 9th grade year, we'll reevaluate the program and make adjustments if necessary. That's the beauty of homeschooling—we can continually make corrections if something isn't working or if we want to go in a different direction. We are not locked into a particular curriculum that may not be providing Mecca with the best education.

All in all, I feel my job during my daughter's high school years is to prepare her for any direction she may want to go after graduation: whether that's attending a four-year university, skating professionally, then going back to college, volunteering abroad or just taking a gap year. Whatever her desires, my goal is that she's ready. During the summer we'll look into possible dual enrollment for her sophomore year which means she can receive high school and college credit simultaneously for the same course. We'll also determine if she'll stay with FLVS or find another program, or maybe a combination of both. We have options, options, options!

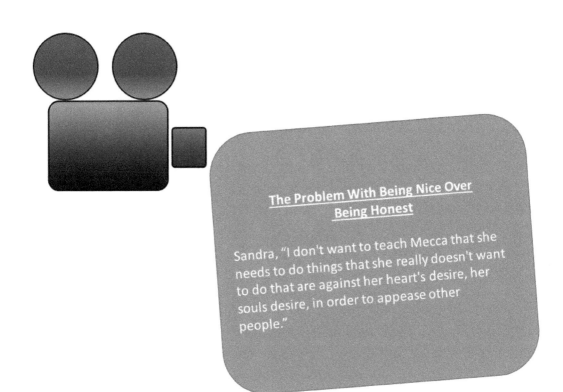

The Problem With Being Nice Over Being Honest

Sandra, "I don't want to teach Mecca that she needs to do things that she really doesn't want to do that are against her heart's desire, her souls desire, in order to appease other people."

Link: https://youtu.be/flZUC0WNMJM

I CAN'T FIND MY DAUGHTER

ven while I searched for my daughter, I knew I was completely overreacting as my heart pounded and lungs contracted. I wanted to scream her name into the crowd, but instead called out, "Mecca! Mecca!" in a controlled, steady voice while striding through the looped foyer hunting for my 12-year-old. I really didn't want to be that crazy mom I had judged who pushed people aside or crawled on hands and knees lifting up table coverings scouring for their lost kid. The ones that had blocked me from leaving a store by demanding security guards lock doors and barricade exits until their child was found. A few people turned to look at me, but most were engaged in talking, laughing and shopping for ice skating apparel. I felt split in two: the rational part that knew my daughter was fine, and my emotional body that burned with the fear of *my child is lost*.

Mecca and I arrived at the ice rink ready to volunteer for the regional skating competition taking place at our home ice arena that has three separate rinks. We picked up our badges from the volunteer desk situated in the lobby of the recreation side where the two smaller rinks are located, and where my daughter skates 2-3 times per week. We then headed to our posts in the 7,000-seat main arena where Mecca has skated in several spring and holiday shows with her group classes. We were stationed in the back area away from the public by the locker rooms and entry ramp leading to the ice—the same place she has lined up before going on the ice for her programs. My job was to line the teams up before their performances, and Mecca's role was to help organize and return the blade guards to the skaters once they got off the ice. In between our duties, we watched the skaters and marveled at the costumes and pageantry. We decided to sit and watch the groups from the stands after we completed our shift.

By this time, we had been at the rink several hours and I was tired and ready to head home.

"I'm going to stop at the bathroom before we go," I said.

"I forgot my jacket by where we were volunteering," Mecca said as we walked through the bustling, loud concourse toward the restrooms.

"Okay. Go get it and meet me back here," I said as she took off through the security barrier to get her coat. We were still wearing our volunteer badges and could access the 'staff only' areas.

I waited patiently outside of the restroom for her to return. She only had to go around the back loop of the concourse 25 yards or so, meaning it shouldn't have taken long. I was hesitant to leave our meeting spot because I didn't want to miss her. The clock ticked on, no sign of my child. Finally, I went to search for her. When I arrived at the ramp entry on the other side, my daughter's jacket was gone and no one had seen her. My heart dropped a bit. I looked around but she wasn't there.

I walked back to the restroom hoping she was waiting for me. No Mecca. She didn't have her cell phone with her, so I couldn't call her.

Tension arose in my chest. *Which way should I go?* I thought.

I headed toward the front of the building where vendors had set up racks of sparkling dresses and fashionable warm-up outfits, and tables full of gloves and trinkets. My head swung left and right trying to find my kid. I was annoyed and tense at the same time: annoyed because I was tired and she hadn't met me where we agreed; tense since she hadn't met me where we agreed, and I didn't know where she was.

Because this was a regional competition, hundreds of people attended that we didn't know. I seldom recognized a face in the crowd, and when I did, I asked them if they had seen my daughter. "No."

Tension grew into mild panic: my heart raced, my breathing shallowed. *Who are these people? Did someone take my daughter? Did she leave? Where is she!* Crazy thoughts entered my mind as my pace quickened.

At the same time, a more rational inner voice spoke as well which kept me from actually screaming her name. *You are out of control, get a grip. Mecca knows this arena, she's fine. She's not a baby anymore. We've been here millions of times, how could she be lost?* I took in deep breaths to calm down while repeating my favorite four-step ancient Hawaiian forgiveness process called ho'oponopono, that Dr. Hew Len, co-author of *Zero Limits*, teaches to release the fear: "I'm Sorry", "Please Forgive Me", "I Love You", "Thank You". This helped tremendously, but I was aware I couldn't fully relax until I found my daughter.

I sped around the whole concourse searching and calling out. I finally reached the glass doors leading to the recreation area and thought, *I bet she went back to the check-in desk.* I bolted through the doors and dashed by the pro shop heading to the lobby. My daughter was there waiting for me by the desk. I almost cried with relief.

"Where were you?" I asked, my voice a bit wobbly.

"I've been waiting for you," she said.

"I told you to meet me outside the bathroom."

"Oh. I didn't hear you. I waited by my jacket, then came over here."

"I've been looking all over for you. I said to meet me at the bathroom. I even pointed to the spot. I waited forever then went to find you."

"I didn't hear you." She stood calmly looking at me, her answer sufficient to her.

"Turn in your badge and let's go," I said sharply. The girl at the desk reached for my badge with a puzzled look but didn't say anything. I was too shaken up to offer an explanation for my abrupt behavior, so I handed it to her quickly and left.

As we walked to the car, I calmed myself down with more deep breathing and ho'oponopono. I was relieved, emotional, and raw. We climbed into the car without speaking, however I wasn't quite ready to let it go. I turned to Mecca in the back seat before pulling out of the parking lot.

"You can't just run off like that. How was I supposed to know you didn't hear me?" I asked.

"I don't know. I thought we were meeting by my jacket."

"Why did you think that?"

"I don't know."

"Well. Well, just make sure you're clear about where we're meeting before you go running off next time. Okay?"

"Okay."

I turned on the radio and we drove home in silence. I bit my tongue because I knew I needed to stop badgering my kid and taking my distress out on her. In the end, she hadn't intentionally dissed me, and she had shown sound judgement by waiting at the volunteer desk.

Over the next few days, I really dug into my forgiveness practice to clear the panic I had experienced. Dr. Len talks about memories replaying in our sub-conscious that are playing out in our lives affecting how we experience people and the world. Ultimately, according to Len, these memories can be erased by practicing ho'oponopono. Deep down, I knew my fear was disproportionate to the situation, even while it was occurring, because my insides had felt like I was digging through rubble looking for loved ones after a bomb explosion. In reality, all that had happened was that I'd lost track of my daughter for a few minutes. I had definitely been reacting to some kind of memory. I didn't know what that memory was, but I had successfully used ho'oponopono for years to heal and forgive other disturbances and knew this was my way to peace and harmony.

I was able to test out the results of my forgiveness work pretty quickly. Shortly thereafter, when I couldn't immediately find Mecca in a department store, my heart didn't completely drop like it had in the past, it was more of a slight skip instead. This was definitely progress! I calmly walked around the clothing racks and found her happily shopping. I didn't say a word about not being able to promptly find her.

I continue to practice ho'oponopono whenever I'm disturbed or fear comes up, not only for my benefit, but for my daughter's as well. When I asked Mecca about the arena incident, she said she never felt like she was lost and hadn't known I was panicked. I continue to forgive all upsets that come my way, because I'd much rather release my personal dread than hinder her life and freedom by burdening her with my unwarranted worries and craziness.

UNAPOLOGETIC

ur indoor mall wasn't too crowded for a Black Friday. My 13-year-old daughter and I had stopped to get smoothies before our shopping excursion, so we slurped on those as we strolled through the center.

"We're supposed to be shopping for bras," Mecca said as I picked up a heather gray sweater outfit. A sheepish grin crossed my face. "We are," I said and continued to look around for other bargains in the large department store.

"I'm going to try these on." I turned and walked toward the fitting rooms. We went into our favorite large room in the back corner—we like to spread out.

"This is so me," I said as I admired the outfit. "Feel how soft it is." Mecca nodded in agreement and took a sip of my smoothie; she had already downed hers.

"Ugh, this tastes good at first, then has a weird aftertaste," she said and belched pretty loud. I ignored her belch, like usual, and tried on a coral sweatsuit. "I like the other one better," Mecca said with her feet propped on the bench, back rested against the wall, scrutinizing my selections.

145

"Hmm, I kind of like them both," I said while posing in the mirror. Another booming bullfrog burp erupted from my daughter, the kind that emanates from a rumbling stomach and explodes uninhibited without regard to its audience; the smoothie wasn't going down well.

"Seriously?" the woman in the adjoining stall shouted. It took me a moment before I realized she was reacting to the objectionable sounds coming from our dressing room—I had thought we were alone in our private alcove. I gasped and looked wide-eyed at Mecca, mouthing that the woman was referring to her. We froze. In the past, I would have apologized for my daughter's offensive behavior, then I would have lowered my voice so as not to disturb anyone. But not that day. I busted out laughing—a deep belly laugh that shook my whole body. Mecca laughed too and we continued our conversation like nothing had happened.

There have been times when I've apologized for my kid cutting someone off because she didn't see them, or she didn't realize someone was trying to get by her, and I gently guided her to the side. However, in that moment, I felt free and uninhibited, hidden by the fitting room walls. I felt free to talk and laugh with my daughter, free to let her be her, obnoxious burps and all. I didn't feel like going on one of my mom rants about burping in public (she knew better, she just got a bit too comfortable) nor did I feel like addressing the woman next to us—I felt bold and unapologetic.

I finally decided on the gray sweater outfit, it would be perfect for our next day trip. It was a bit dressier than the coral sweatsuit and would look better with my boots. We gathered the clothes and started to leave, then paused and cracked the door to make sure the hall was clear before running out of the fitting room, back to the main shopping area to quickly blend in with the rest of the shoppers. I may have been feeling bold, but I didn't want to be identified by the woman next door, especially since we were still giggling like two school girls on the playground and not taking it seriously at all.

IT ALL STARTED WITH THE ICE CREAM

y 9-year-old daughter was unusually still on the back bench of our minivan during our New Year's Day drive from Atlanta back to Southwest Florida.

"Is she okay?" Thomas asked yet again.

"Yeah, I think so. She's breathing," I said.

"What's wrong with her?"

"I don't know. I guess she's tired," I answered. He always assumed I had all the answers just because I'm the mom. I tuned into my intuition to see if I could get any clues about what was going on. I received nothing specific other than she needed to rest.

We were about four to five hours into our twelve-hour drive and Mecca had not said a word or shifted her position.

"Mecca, we're stopping to eat. Can you wake up and put your shoes on please?" I called to her.

"Huh?"

"We're stopping. Put your shoes on," Thomas repeated.

"I'm not hungry," she groaned.

"You can't stay in the car. Put your shoes on," I said.

As we pulled into our favorite roadside chain restaurant, Mecca slowly awoke, barely. She didn't eat anything and held her head up by leaning on the palm of her hand during lunch. We'd never seen her like this and couldn't figure out if she was exhausted or sick. We had hung out with friends the evening before celebrating New Year's Eve—lighting fireworks and eating dessert, but her disposition was out of character.

Finally, after concerned questioning from us, she grumbled, "I think I ate too much sugar last night."

"What did you eat?" we asked.

"I don't know. Cupcakes, s'mores, candy. I don't remember exactly."

"Oh, so you're in a sugar coma," I said. The little knots in my stomach relaxed, relieved to discover why she was acting half-dead.

She closed her eyes, folded her arms on the table, laid her head down and retreated back into her own inner world, ignoring further comments and questions from us about her sugar intake.

Mecca slept the rest of the drive home. We left her alone. She had a mild fever that night and most of the next day. Her body was hard at work expelling the sugar like it would a virus or bacterium that attacked it. You can tell a kid over and over not to stick their finger in a light socket, but the quickest deterrent is the sharp shock of electrical current stinging the tip of their finger then shooting up their arm. This was Mecca's shock.

When Mecca turned 11, we decided to let her regulate her sugar intake. Each year brought about new freedoms and responsibilities, so this seemed like a natural progression to us. Prior to that, she had one dessert per day (except on special occasions like New Year's Eve), and water was her primary beverage. This actually seemed a bit hypocritical since I grew up eating tons of sugar. We added sugar to our sugary cereal. We made Kool-Aid drink mix with twice as much sugar as the recommended amount. I chewed sugared bubblegum every day, all day, drank soda and devoured loads of candy. You get the picture. Times were different then—most people we knew ate as much or more sweets than we did.

I was a bit hesitant to let go of control, but it felt fitting to allow her to make this food choice. By this time, she knew the negative impact of excessive sugar on her body and we had discussed eating habits to support vibrant health and stamina for years. We had friends on both ends of the sugar spectrum: those who closely monitored their kids' sugar with a microscope, and a few who had soda with every meal. We were somewhere in between.

My daughter was surprised by her new freedom. At first Thomas and I would catch ourselves trying to restrict her diet when we'd see her eating cookies, then candy and maybe an additional sugary treat. She would gently (not really) remind us this was her choice. I occasionally wondered if we were being negligent parents by letting her eat all the sweets she wanted—she was only 11, after all.

There were times that I actually cringed watching her stuff a handful of Halloween candy into her mouth. I would reminisce out loud about breast-feeding her exclusively for one year, then preparing home-made organic baby food until she was two, extolling the dedication and commitment I had put forth to provide her with a healthy, clean diet. She was unimpressed and continued indulging happily in her sweet treats, although never to the point of inducing another sugar coma.

As Dr. W. pushed on Mecca's stomach, he asked her, "How is your diet and sugar intake?"

"They're good," she said and looked over to me for confirmation.

"She could eat less sugar," I said. Dr. W. is a Sacro Occipital Technique (SOT) chiropractor, which is a unique combination of chiropractic and osteopathy that not only works on aligning one's spine, but finds imbalances in the body. He was feeling inflammation in Mecca's gut.

"How about dairy? Do you eat a lot of cheese and ice cream and things with milk in them?" he asked.

"Sort of," she answered.

"Hmm, you should cut down on foods that have a lot of sugar and dairy because they cause inflammation and gas and ultimately create imbalances in your body," he said.

"Oh."

I had been taking Mecca to the SOT chiropractor once a month for over a year to keep her aligned, since she regularly falls on hard ice while practicing her jumps and spins ice skating. Dr. W. adjusts her knees, ankles, hips, back and neck, in addition to balancing her stomach, intestines and major internal organs. Each time we go he tries to dissuade her from her sweet tooth. She nods in agreement, but I think that's just to get him to stop talking about her diet.

A few months ago, I noticed I hadn't bought any ice cream for my 14-year-old daughter. Whenever I picked up my favorite non-dairy brand, she would decline her beloved cookies and cream.

"No, it makes me too gassy," she said.

Next, I realized I hadn't bought any cut-and-bake chocolate chip cookies or Oreos for weeks. I was buying carrots, apples, almond yogurts and chips for her snacks. And she didn't always finish her salted dark chocolate caramel filled candy bar at the movies anymore. In the past she had devoured the whole bar in one sitting. Now she often had several squares left over.

"I reduced my sugar," Mecca announced while we prepared dinner one evening.

"Why?" Thomas asked.

"Because I wanted to," was her short answer. I just rolled my eyes at Thomas knowing we weren't going to get more from her until she was ready.

A couple of days later the subject came up again and she was more forthcoming with her answer.

"I realized that I was not going to exercise enough to counterbalance the amount of sugar I was eating, so I decided to cut back on my sugar," she said.

"Wow, that's pretty insightful," I said.

"Yep!"

"Well, how do you feel?" I asked.

"Good," she said.

"Do you notice a difference in your skating or thinking?"

"I have more stamina now. I can do more with less energy. I used to be dead after two hours of skating, now I'm fine. I feel stronger and less sluggish. And I've thinned down and toned up. I have more energy overall."

I swelled with pride that she had come to this decision all on her own.

"It all started with the cones," she continued about her process. "My milk sensitivity grew to where I couldn't eat ice cream in large quantities and Dr. W. told me to cut down. I got tired of eating Oreos and daddy stopped buying random desserts so there was less stuff in the house. Then, most of the time I was too lazy to bake the cookies and I realized I didn't miss them."

"Cool, but the ice cream has been making you gassy for a while and Dr. W. said something to you months ago."

"I know but I didn't care," she said.

"I think it's great that you came to this on your own."

"I'm very wise." She smiled.

I've learned over the years that everything is a phase with Mecca. Will she permanently reduce her sugar consumption? Who knows? But the fact that she has the discipline and awareness to consciously choose for herself moment to moment warms my heart. The years of shoveling sugar down her throat gave her the experience of feeling lethargic and out of shape. Now she's choosing to feel clear and strong. Ultimately, it's her life, her body and her consequences to live with. So, for now, I'm doing the happy dance that she's cut back on her sugar without me or Thomas having to badger her about it.

ICE BREAKERS:

Parents: Do you let your kids self-regulate their diet? Why or why not?

Kids: What kind of food choices would you make if your parents let you self-regulate your diet?

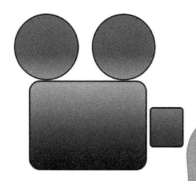

Are You Imposing Your Unfulfilled Desires Onto Your Child?

Sandra and Thomas, "You squash those dreams...and then it pops up with your child because it doesn't go away it just kind of recycles and then all of a sudden you're pushing your kid to do something that they have no interest in...they try to please you or you get a lot of pushback and then you start calling them difficult."

Link: https://youtu.be/KjTMDli5Gig

SLEEP IS HER FRIEND

My 14-year-old daughter has decided to sleep her way through the COVID-19 global pandemic. She's always been a night owl, but recently my husband started teasing her about being a vampire. "When will Mecca rise?" is our new joke. Usually, it's been before sunset.

I used to worry about leaving her alone for too long. Occasionally she would call and ask when we'd be home because she was feeling a bit lonely. Now, Thomas and I can go for a late morning bike ride or kayaking, stop for a smoothie and arrive home before she even bats an eye. Is a teenager really able to snooze until 3:30 in the afternoon? You betcha!

At Mecca's last chiropractic visit, her doctor noticed she had lost weight. I assumed she was losing muscle mass from not skating, but he explained that she's going through her secondary developmental stage. *What?*

"She's getting curvier and stretching out," he said.

Oh, so that's why she's suddenly taller than me, I thought.

When I did a tad of research on sleep requirements for teens, I found additional information on secondary development from Hopkins pediatrician Michael Crocetti, M.D., M.P.H. (Crocetti, Michael. "Sleep Tips For Teenagers." 27 Feb 2020, *Alaska Sleep Clinic,* https://www.alaskasleep.com/blog/sleep-tips-for-teenagers.*)* He states,

"Teens need 9 to 9½ hours of sleep per night—that's an hour or so *more* than they needed at age 10. Why? Teenagers are going through a second developmental stage of cognitive maturation. Additional sleep supports their developing brain, as well as physical growth spurts."

Well, my daughter is averaging 12-13 hours per night, so her brain development is surely working overtime.

This is the perfect opportunity for Mecca to get an abundance of rest, since all of her activities are on hold because of the worldwide virus outbreak. I'm usually in bed by 1:30am while she's still wide-awake in her room painting tiny canvases, listening to music, organizing her shelves and books, making miniature clay flower pots, playing with her hamster Chewy, or watching Netflix until two or three in the morning.

As a competitive ice skater, my daughter skates four to eight hours a week and does gymnastics and off-ice workouts, so not being able to skate and train has been disappointing for her. Fortunately, because the rink is closed and upcoming competitions have been canceled, she's not falling behind, since no one else can skate either.

After her spring break was over, I requested that my daughter bike ride with me at least three times a week so she wouldn't be too out of shape when it's time to get back on the ice; she enthusiastically agreed—not! Once she's up and on the bike she's in good spirits; it's getting her out of bed before noon that takes some negotiating and patience. We ride anywhere from four to eight miles and often pick up lunch while we're out. Thomas does stomach crunches with her nightly before dinner and I've seen her ankle weights in the middle of her bedroom floor; some exercise is much better than no exercise at all.

Overall, I think my daughter is handling isolation and social distancing very well, especially for an active teenager. Since we homeschool, we didn't have to make a huge transition in her weekly school work and she's been completing her assignments on time. We play board games, go for evening walks and watch movies. With all this in mind, if she wants to sleep until late afternoon to deal with this pandemic, then so be it.

THE SANDWICH WAS THE FINAL STRAW

was stunned as I watched my 13-year-old daughter pull her homemade turkey and cheese sandwich out from her Kiss and Cry tote and casually lean against the side board of the ice rink to nibble it down. She took a bite, chewed, took another bite, drank some water, and stood idly watching the other ice skaters practice while she munched on her lunch. *What the hell is she doing?* I thought. I was in the lobby looking at her through the large glass window, so she didn't see my brows furrow and my building agitation.

Of course, I don't want my child to starve, and of course she needs energy to practice her jumps and spins, but really, she should have eaten the sandwich before she got on the ice.

Mecca loved going to the rink at least twice a week, three to four times a week before a competition, and usually skated for at least two freestyle sessions each day; so, she was skating 4-8 hours a week. It was great physical training, but it was also a social time for her. She had gotten into the habit of chatting with her friends when she arrived at the rink instead of stretching and preparing to skate.

Freestyle sessions were intended for figure skaters to practice their jumps, spins, routines and advanced skills and differed from public skate sessions which were more recreational. Each freestyle hour cost $12. When she had private lessons, the cost increased quite a bit. When she dawdled before getting on the ice, I became annoyed.

That morning, I had cut my bicycle ride short to take my kid to the rink. It was a 20-minute drive, more than enough time for Mecca to have eaten her sandwich in the car. When we walked into the lobby of the arena, her friend was there waiting for public skate to start on the opposite rink. Instead of stretching, Mecca chit-chatted. I watched the clock.

I really don't like being a pushy mom, but I finally interrupted their conversation and said, "Mecca your session is starting."

"Oh, okay." She tied her skates and hustled toward the ice. Five minutes late.

The week before she was chatting with another friend and was late starting her freestyle session.

"What are you doing?" I asked her, pointing to the clock.

"I'm going, I'm going." She hurried to put on her skates. "I'm only five minutes late," she said over her shoulder as she rushed to the ice.

Another time she was almost late for her private lesson. I calculated the cost per minute of her coach's time and ice time she was wasting and showed her— $1.33 per minute.

"Oh," she said. I thought by her startled expression she understood the point I was trying to make about getting her butt on the ice when the session started, not five or ten minutes late.

On this particular afternoon, not only was Mecca late getting on the ice, she spent an inordinate amount of time re-tying her skates on the side bench, fiddling with her water bottle, blowing her nose, and piddle-paddling before skating. She took just one lap, then stopped to eat her sandwich. I checked the clock; she had wasted about 15 minutes.

I was tired of getting upset by her behavior and decided I needed a better strategy than grumbling about her tardiness. As she skated, I plotted...

156

As soon as she finished skating, and before she even removed her blades, I said, "I feel like you're being very cavalier about getting on the ice on time."

"What does cavalier mean?" I handed her my cell phone. I had already pulled up the definition. She frowned as she read it.

Cavalier: showing a lack of proper concern; offhand.

"I feel like you're showing a lack of proper concern for the money we are spending on your freestyle sessions." I used the words from the dictionary to drive my point home. She was silent. I then recounted all the non-skating activity she did during the freestyle session she had just completed.

"I was hungry," she said as an excuse about the sandwich.

"Why didn't you eat in the car if you were so hungry?"

"I wasn't hungry then." I rolled my eyes but didn't get upset because I had a plan.

"I'm tired of complaining about this," I said. "Tomorrow you're going to pay for your ice time. So whatever t-shirt, pin, or Funko Pop you were going to buy at Hot Topic, forget about it. You're paying for your ice, then you can piddle-paddle all you want."

"That's mean," she said.

"I think it's fair."

"Humph." She turned abruptly and stalked away. I grinned at my victory.

* * *

The next day, Mecca insisted we arrive 30 minutes before her freestyle session started. She handed me her $20 bill and asked me to pay because she didn't want to waste time standing in line at the cashier. This time, instead of chatting with her friend, they stretched and warmed up together. I noticed she was watching the clock to stay on track. She had her skates on and headed to the ice a minute before the session started—I didn't have to say a word, or be the pushy mom. I smiled to myself, relaxed and chatted with the other parents.

If my daughter slips back into acting cavalier, I won't pester her, I'll just have her pay out of her own money again. That way she feels the burn in her pocket of those wasted minutes ticking away, not me.

THE PRESUMPTION OF RACE

"Your daughter should really come down and hang out when the teens from the NAACP (National Association for the Advancement of Colored People) are here," a board member said to me during a meeting at our predominantly white Unitarian Universalist church. I'm one of few people of color there.

"Hmm," I murmured.

"The kids have a blast out here on the patio. They play their music and break into spoken word, dance and poetry," they continued.

"Oh," I feigned interest. It's not that it was a bad idea, I just didn't think my daughter would be interested. My biracial 14-year-old can recite the lyrics to Broadway musicals like *Dear Evan Hanson* and *Hamilton*, ice skates and doesn't know a bit of black slang. She stopped watching the TV show *Blackish* because she didn't understand the cultural references. Just because she's brown-skinned, doesn't mean she likes the same things as others do that look like her.

"That's the problem with pushing people to study their ancestry," my husband blurted out after thinking about the incident. We had just launched our inflatable kayaks on the jungle-like river that reminds us of an ancient Mayan city in Mexico that we love when I told him about my experience that morning. Mecca was sleeping in, so it was just the two of us.

"What do you mean?"

"Well, you box people into a story. You're following a line that takes you to a dead end because it doesn't take you to being Spirit. It doesn't lead you to being a direct download of the Divine," he said.

"Damn! That's good, Honey." I thought about what he said as we paddled up the river. The beauty and essence of the water, mangroves, live oaks and bamboo trees always calmed my mind. I definitely felt like the board member had boxed my daughter into a story without even knowing it, and I was riled up about it.

⁂

I've always told my daughter I want her to be a citizen of the world. I want her to be comfortable and confident wherever she goes and to feel like anything and everything is available for her life. We travel as much as possible, first, because we love to, and second, because we want to expose her to as many types of people and places as possible. One of my proudest moments was watching her keenly navigate the subway system in Paris last year and direct us to several hip spots around the city. Other times I've brimmed with joy seeing her climb up the ruins of Tikal, Guatemala and Palenque, Mexico. I certainly didn't travel like this when I was a kid.

Sometimes, I wonder if she's missing out on other things. Her upbringing is so much different from mine, but is one better than the other? I had barbecues and card parties; she travels and goes to cultural events. I grew up around people of all races in Southern California. I had black neighbors and Hispanic neighbors, white friends and black friends. I went to college and lived in Los Angeles for 30 plus years, the melting pot of the region. There were Thai restaurants, Ethiopian eateries, Jewish delis and Soul Food joints all around the city.

Even with all this diversity, I remember going to a family reunion with my uncle, aunt and cousins and feeling completely out of place. I had nothing in common with the people there—in my semi-preppy garb and matching attitude, I stuck out like a sore thumb amongst my inner-city relatives. My initial excitement about meeting new family members turned into utter disappointment. I had presumed blood and race would bond us—they didn't.

I fault myself for my child not knowing any black slang. I speak some slang around my close black girlfriends, like stretching out 'girl' to 'girrrlll' to add emphasis to a point I'm making, but in general, I don't. I sometimes wonder if she is growing up without a culture, without any racial identity. Is being mixed-raced an identity? Does it even matter?

"Does it bother you that you don't know any black slang? That you didn't know what 'Yo face is tore up from the floor up' meant?" I asked Mecca, referring to a blotchy rash all over her face.

"No, I'm not around a lot of black people and that was the first time you ever said that to me, so I'm not really worried about it," she said. It often seems like the things I trip over in my mind, my daughter could care less about.

My white husband teases me about being *L.A. Black,* which to him means a unique style of black person. I don't think speaking Ebonics and knowing slang makes one person blacker than another. Whatever.

When we lived in Atlanta, most of Mecca's friends were black. Now that we're in Southwest Florida, most of them are white. She doesn't care what race they are, as long as they're nice; she loves sleepovers and hanging out, friends are friends.

"How do you decide who you want to talk to at camp?" I once asked her.

"I observe people until I find someone who looks interesting," she said.

"Interesting how?"

"I hear them talk about something I like or maybe they have on a shirt from a show I watch. Something interesting."

When we first moved to Southwest Florida I stated, "I want to find a black female friend."

My daughter asked simply, "What difference does their color make?"

"Well, sometimes I feel like I can be more myself, or there's a shared experience that's unspoken that we can bond over.

"I just look for people that I have something in common with," she said. I felt her perspective was definitely a better place to come from, but I still wanted my black friend.

As we neared the ramp to pull our kayaks from the water, my husband called out, "We are teaching Mecca about her ancestry."

160

"Say more," I encouraged.

"Well, we're teaching her that she is the image and likeness of God. That's all that really matters. Everything else is a story." It was like he could hear my internal struggle.

"Yeah, you're right." Once again, paddling on our favorite mystical river had cleared and calmed my mind enough to receive reflective answers. I thought back to a couple of years ago when Mecca said she knew she was part of something bigger. She didn't call it God, but she knew she was connected to everything in the Universe.

What my daughter has already figured out for herself is that shared interests and values, similar backgrounds and philosophies create bonds and friendships that are not defined by the color of her skin. She doesn't presume that she will mesh with someone just because they may look similar to her.

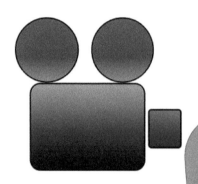

How To Teach Your New Age Kid To Avoid Experiencing A Mean and Cruel World

Sandra and Thomas, "What I put out there is coming back to me. And you can test this out by just putting something out there and seeing when it comes back...you don't have to rely on faith, you just become a detective of your own personal behavior and attitude and see what comes right back to you. You can change it in an instant."

THE PRESUMPTION OF RACE: MY EXPERIENCE AND THOUGHTS ABOUT BEING BIRACIAL

WRITTEN BY MECCA JONES-KELLER

or most of my life, I wasn't aware of or concerned about things that happened to me because of the color of my skin and my curly hair. It wasn't until I got older and moved to a mostly white town that I began to realize just how different I technically was from most of the people around me. This led me to having to work through my insecurities about myself. Ultimately, I had to stop caring so much about what others thought of me.

From as young as I can remember, my hair has always been the center of attention when it comes to my appearance. I have curly brown hair and used to wear it down a lot when I was younger, but started wearing it up as I got older because I got tired of people touching and messing with it without my permission. Many, many, many times throughout my entire life people have always wanted to touch and play with my hair, whether it was because they were admiring it, or were just curious about it. Unfortunately for them, I don't like my hair being touched, but that rarely mattered since they would touch it anyway

163

or beg me to let them touch it until I gave in. I also don't like my hair touched because it takes a long time to get it looking nice. Above all, it made me feel like I was an animal at a petting zoo or some "exotic" exhibit for people to look at.

Some people would say things like "OMG, I love your hair, I wish my hair was like that!" or "I would give anything for my hair to look like that." What they don't know is that curly hair takes a lot of work to manage and care for and 90% of the time it doesn't actually look like what they see or think it looks like. Tons of conditioner, hair creams, gels, brushes, combs and most importantly, time go into making what people think curly hair looks like. Having perfect curly hair is a fantasy that people with straight hair don't understand and probably wouldn't want to actually put in the work for. They were born with hair that generally can be managed fairly easily (I've braided and styled several of my friends' hair) and they don't have to deal with the struggle trying to tame it, not to mention all the lost and broken hair ties and stuck combs.

Straight-haired people fawning over my hair led to me having very strong desires to have straight hair. However, it wasn't until we moved to our current state that my desire to have straight hair evolved from not wanting it to be touched to wanting to look like the other kids around me. Living in Atlanta, I was mostly surrounded by people who looked similar to me in terms of hair texture and skin color, but when we moved to a predominantly white area, I felt ostracized and alone. Thus began my desire of wishing I had straight hair so that I could blend in and be "a part of the community."

I started wearing my hair up so that it wasn't obvious that it was different from everyone else's. If I did wear it down, I felt insecure and uncomfortable, which is why my parents and friends rarely saw it down. I've had friends try to style and comb through my hair without much luck—it would just end up tangled and frizzy, which didn't help my situation.

At 12 years old, I chopped off most of my hair because I had bleached it so many times it was very dry, and I felt it would make me stand out less. During that time, I experimented with different hair colors (pinks, purples and blues) and styles which made me feel more comfortable because people would pay more attention to the color than my actual hair texture.

Now that I'm 15 and more secure with myself, I am growing my hair out, because I want to experience long hair without the previous insecurities I had about it.

Another change/insecurity that developed from moving was about my body type. I'm pretty muscular with a somewhat large chest, hips and thighs, but I have a small waist which has made finding clothing I'm comfortable in and that fit quite challenging. The body type here is mostly skinny girls with fewer curves than black or even mixed people. I've gotten used to wearing what I can find and have come to personalize and like my own style of clothing.

There's also a struggle when it comes to my body type and my sport, figure skating. The figure skating community is dominated by slim, graceful girls and although there is definitely more diversity than there used to be, the number of people of color is still pretty low. This has led me to feel somewhat alone, since most of the people at my skating rink are white and have a different skating style from me. Also, I'm not a very gentle skater which has made it a bit challenging for me to find music that fits my style and rhythm. In addition, finding skating dresses that fit properly has been a big issue. They are either too big in the chest, too short in the back, or just too small in all the places where I have curves.

Next, there is the issue of people attempting to pronounce my name. Personally, I don't think my name is that difficult, since it sounds very similar to other names, but I find most people cannot pronounce it correctly. Most of the time when people struggle, I don't find it to be connected to the fact that I am biracial, but there have been a few instances where I felt it might have been.

In the end, I am very fortunate that I haven't experienced any harsh racism or hate crimes due to the fact that I'm biracial, but I'm sure many other kids like me have had similar things happen to them simply because they are somewhat different from others. I am now a lot more comfortable with myself and my hair because I have learned that it doesn't do me any good to worry about what others think of me. The only thoughts that truly matter are my own, and that the people who really want to be my friend will accept me and my wishes, and for that I will ultimately live a better life.

TOO MUCH JUICE

"The celery juice is really clearing up your skin," I marveled for the hundredth time while looking at my 14-year-old daughter's face.

"It's not helping that much," she said.

"What do you mean? Your skin is looking great."

"Well, I haven't really been drinking it."

"Huh? Daddy's been bringing it up to you for the past couple of weeks. What do you mean you haven't been drinking it?"

"I only drink half and throw the rest out."

My eyebrows shot up in shock. "Half?"

"Yeah, it hurts my stomach. He gives me too much."

"Oooh, I'm telling Daddy."

"What are you, five?"

"Yep! He's gone to a lot of trouble to make and bring that juice to you every morning. Then you throw out half. He's not going to be happy."

She shrugged her shoulders and remained silent, a typical response for her. I ran downstairs to tattle on Mecca, but Thomas was outside washing down the lanai, so I started dinner. She followed me and waited for him as well. I guess she figured she wanted to tell her side of the story before I disclosed what she'd been doing.

✻ ✻ ✻

Five months ago, Mecca woke up one morning with an itchy rash on the left side of her face. There were light, fuzzy patches above her eye, on her cheek and chin. It looked as if she had laid her face on something that irritated her skin, but she hadn't been anywhere the day before so we were stumped.

I checked with my health guru Louise Hay. According to her book, *Heal Your Body: The Mental Causes for Physical Illness and the Metaphysical Way to Overcome Them,* rashes indicate irritation over delays. My heart sank...all of my daughter's activities had been delayed and/or cancelled due to the COVID-19 global pandemic. She had been coping pretty well for the first couple of months by sleeping late and busying herself around the house, but she was ready to get back to ice skating and seeing her friends, and the delays were taking a toll on her body.

I contacted my doTERRA essential oil consultant who suggested making a blend of tea tree, peppermint, lavender, lemon and geranium oils in a base of fractionated coconut oil for my daughter to apply on her face twice daily. We waited excitedly thinking her skin would clear up quickly, but it actually spread to the right side of her face and down her left leg.

At her next regular appointment, we asked her SOT chiropractor to examine the rash; he thought it was stress and food related, given we were in the middle of a global pandemic. He muscled-tested her for food sensitivities which showed she was sensitive to white flour and gluten—she'd been doing A LOT of baking to keep busy—so she cut out her tasty treats, but her rash didn't improve.

After a month of no progress, we took my daughter in to see the owner of the chiropractic office, who has over 20 years' experience, and has a broader expertise than her regular chiropractor. She looked at Mecca's face and immediately said, "This looks like tinea versicolor."

"What's that?" I asked.

"It's a common fungal infection. It can happen when the liver is over-stressed and the gut isn't working properly."

She did adjustments to strengthen Mecca's liver and digestive system and gave her supplements to repair her gut. In addition, she recommended my daughter drink peppermint and lemon oils mixed with honey and water each morning to detox her liver, while continuing to use the essential oil blend twice daily directly on the rash. We left her office feeling hopeful since we had a prognosis and treatment plan. She warned us the rash might worsen before it improved as her body detoxed.

She wasn't joking. My poor kid broke out with severe acne and the rash spread to her right underarm and both legs. *Holy shit, will this thing ever heal*, I thought. The funny thing is, Thomas and I seemed to be more concerned about the outbreak than Mecca was. She was taking it all in stride. Fortunately, she had nowhere to go which I think made it easier for her to deal with.

Each day we examined her face looking for improvements—very little, and very slowly, but at least it wasn't getting worse. My husband took pictures to track her progress. After a couple of visits, the doctor was extremely happy with the strength of my daughter's liver and gut and okayed her to do a stronger detox.

※ ※ ※

Thomas had been reading about the benefits of celery juice from various sources. Some of the benefits include:

✓ Healing the gut and relieving digestive disorders.

✓ Balancing blood sugar, blood pressure, weight, and adrenal function.

✓ Providing the brain with critical electrolyte support to counter disease.

✓ Neutralizing and flushing toxins from the liver and brain.

He was so impressed with the testimonials of improved health and digestive balance from this miracle juice that he decided to do a cleanse with it for himself, and was thrilled that Mecca and I agreed to do it with him. We had no idea if it would clear up her rash, but figured we would all benefit from a cleaner liver.

My hubby went to the store a few times a week to purchase the supplies. Each morning he brought us both a glass of water with freshly squeezed organic lemons followed by 12-16 ounces of freshly made organic celery juice twenty minutes later. 16 ounces was the recommended amount for optimal results, however, I varied the amounts depending on how my stomach felt.

We were ecstatic when Mecca's rash began to disappear quickly once she started on the celery juice cleanse. Maybe it was a combination of all the things she had been doing, but the results were undeniable; her face looked the best it had in months. So, when Mecca admitted to throwing out half of her juice, I was shocked and I knew my husband would be upset due to all the effort he put into it every morning.

"Mecca has something she wants to tell you," I said as I jumped in from across the kitchen pass-through as Thomas opened the front door. She was sitting at the dining room table waiting for him while I prepared dinner.

"What?" he asked her. He was hot and sticky from being outside and reached for a towel to dry off.

"I haven't been drinking all of the celery juice," she said.

"What do you mean? Your glass is empty when I pick it up from your room?"

"I drink half and throw half of it out."

"Why do you do that?"

"Because it makes me feel horrible."

"You feel horrible because your body is in bad condition and you're cleaning it out. I feel fine. Where do you throw it out, because I'm downstairs?"

"In your bathroom sink."

"So, you get up out of bed, go to the bathroom and throw it away, then get back in bed?" he asked in disbelief.

He looked at me. "Did you know about this?"

"Nope. I just found out a few minutes ago and came down to tell you."

"Why didn't you say something before?" he asked her.

"I did, and I've left some in the glass and you woke me up and made me drink the rest of it, so I started throwing it out."

"I thought you'd want to drink it since your face is clearing up so quickly now."

"Which is why I kept drinking it, but not all of it."

"You lied about drinking it and I've just been wasting money."

"I never said that I'd been drinking all of it."

"You led me to believe you were drinking all of it. Well, that's half of your allowance for next month," Thomas blurted out.

"Why?" she asked.

"Because that's how much it costs for the juice you threw out. Mommy or I could have been drinking it. You just wasted 25 dollars' worth of juicing stuff. Those are the consequences."

I knew his feelings were hurt so I was giving him time to sort through what she had just told him without objection to his proposed punishment. His suggestion didn't feel right to me, but we would talk about it later if he stuck to his decision. She didn't say anything.

We had a quiet meal...after dinner the discussion continued in the living room.

"I didn't tell you guys that I was throwing it out because you were constantly talking about how amazing it was and kept insisting that I drink it, despite me telling you that it makes me feel sick multiple times," Mecca said.

"No. You didn't. You didn't communicate clearly," he said as he shook his head.

PLAY. We started a movie—the room felt chilly from the tension in the air. No one talked.

I thought back to conversations we had with Mecca about the celery juice. PAUSE.

"She did say something to us," I said. "On more than one occasion I remember her saying *I would rather my rash take longer to heal than have a stomach ache from the juice.* We just weren't listening."

"Yep!" she chimed in. I gave her a *'don't be a smartass'* look.

PLAY. Movie over. Exit to separate corners to regroup.

"I still don't know how I feel about what Mecca did," Thomas said while getting ready for bed.

"Hmm." I nodded. After a moment...

"Mecca, can you come here?" I called out.

"Have a seat." I gestured for her to come into the bedroom instead of lingering in the doorway.

"Do you think there was a better way you could have handled this?" I asked her.

"I don't know."

"Well think about it," I said. "How did you feel, throwing it out?"

She sat and finally shrugged her shoulders. "I don't know. I felt pressure not to tell you guys because you kept talking about how good it is for me."

"What, peer pressure?" Thomas asked.

"No, peers are people your age," she said.

Thomas and I looked at each other trying to figure this out. "Parent pressure?" I asked her.

"Yes."

"You have to make sure you speak up for yourself and say when something isn't working," Thomas said to her.

"I have a request," I interrupted. I looked at Mecca.

"What?"

"If, in the future, you feel that we're not hearing you, then write us a note like you've done before. I know you like to communicate in writing," I said. In the past, Mecca has written us notes when she wanted to tell us something important, or if she was upset and wanted to explain her position and feelings. As she has put it, *I don't like to talk about my feelings.*

"And when you write a note, we know that it's serious," Thomas said.

"That way you can make sure we understand what you're trying to tell us. Will you do that?" I asked.

"Yes," she said.

"Thomas, how does that sound to you?"

"That sounds like a great idea!" he said.

"Okay then." She went back to her bedroom and Thomas went to sleep.

As with many of our family conversations, this one unraveled over a couple of days. During breakfast the next morning, Thomas asked Mecca, "So, if I had come upstairs while you were pouring out your juice, would you have felt strong?"

"What do you mean?"

"Just that. Would you have stopped doing it if I came upstairs and saw you? Did you feel strong?"

"Yeah, I guess," she said.

"I disagree," he said.

"So do I," I said. "If you had felt strong and powerful, you wouldn't have hidden it. You timed it so that me or Daddy didn't see you."

"Huh," she murmured.

"Whenever I feel like I have to hide something, I don't feel good. This is about you and your life. You have a powerful life by making powerful choices day to day. Even if we didn't know, you still knew what you were doing," I said.

"Yep," Thomas agreed.

There was a pause in the conversation and she jumped up to wash the dishes and load the dishwasher. I think we were all pretty done with this topic and it was time to move on.

In the end, Thomas rescinded his threat to withhold half her allowance because that didn't make sense to him after our conversations. For some, the solution may have been to punish Mecca for hiding her disposal of the juice, but for me, this would have been akin to taking her to an allopathic doctor and getting a prescription without ever getting to the root cause. Additionally, we would have missed an opportunity for growth and understanding—and ultimately, it's important for Thomas and I, as parents, to foster an environment where our daughter feels safe to stand up for herself, even if initially we don't hear her or disagree.

TOO MUCH JUICE, MY SIDE

WRITTEN BY MECCA JONES-KELLER

One day during quarantine for COVID-19, my mom and I were out for our bike ride when she noticed patches of light-colored areas on my face. I hadn't noticed them before, so when she took a picture and showed me, I was surprised to see a light patch above my eyebrow about an inch and a half wide, along with smaller areas of discoloration. I didn't know what had caused them, or what would make them go away, I only knew that they weren't life threatening, so I wasn't very concerned about them. Although, when she asked what I thought we should do about them, I suggested going to my SOT chiropractor since he was basically my doctor and would have a high chance of helping me.

My chiropractor wasn't exactly sure what it was, but he suspected it was some kind of fungal infection. Since he wasn't sure how to treat it, I started seeing the head chiropractor. She was able to diagnose that it was caused by my liver, coupled with a gluten allergy that hadn't been very prevalent until now, since I had been doing a lot of baking with white flour to fill the time of being inside. She gave me some supplements and a detox program to clean and strengthen my liver. But, even though my liver had gotten stronger, the light patches had spread to more of my face and to my legs.

This was when my dad suggested that I start a lemon water and celery juice cleanse that he and my mom had been doing. After my chiropractor approved it, every morning my dad would bring me a full glass of water with fresh lemon juice, followed 20 minutes later with a tall glass of celery juice. Unfortunately, the celery juice caused me to feel very sick and have terrible stomach aches. Even though it was quickly clearing up my skin, the effects it had on me internally were much worse than having the light areas on my skin, which were only occasionally itchy and didn't give me any trouble.

I told my parents that the celery juice was making me feel sick and that I would rather have the skin discoloration than drink the juice. I felt that my concerns were not heard due to my parents being too thrilled about my skin clearing up. Once, I even left some juice in the glass because I was in too much discomfort to finish it, but I was forced to drink it anyway, further making me feel worse.

After multiple failed attempts of trying to get my parents to listen and understand what I was saying, I knew I had to take things into my own hands. Since I couldn't figure out anything else to do, I started secretly pouring out the celery juice. I only drank what I could manage since it was helping my skin. I immediately felt better. I was able to get up in the morning without an unbearable stomach ache, and in the meantime, my skin was almost completely cleared up. For this reason, I didn't feel very bad about throwing out the juice that my dad made fresh every morning. My parents had always taught me to be self-responsible, and if something wasn't working for me, to take charge and take care of it, which is exactly what I did.

As a result of my skin quickly getting better, my parents started talking more and more about how amazing the celery juice was. Almost every day, I had to listen to my parents go on and on about how fast and efficient the celery juice was working. But, I knew I wasn't actually drinking as much as they thought I was.

After listening to them talk about it constantly for a couple of weeks, I finally got fed up and told my mom I hadn't actually been drinking all of the juice. She was surprised, asked why I did it, then acted like a 5-year-old about to tell on someone, saying, "I'm gonna tell Daddy. He's gonna to be mad." Before she could tattle on me, I tattled on myself. I ran downstairs and told my dad what I had told my mom. He was even more surprised and asked me questions about it.

I explained how bad the celery juice made me feel, but that I still drank about half of it because I knew it was clearing up the light areas. Additionally, I explained how I had tried to tell him before, but neither of them had listened. He was clearly upset. He called me a liar, which I disputed. I told him that I had never said I was actually drinking all of the juice. He then said I misled him, and I agreed with that. I was aware of my actions and the effects they would have, but at that point, all I cared about was being able to get up in the morning without feeling terrible.

Eventually, we all settled down and watched a movie. After the movie, I was in my bedroom when I was called into my parent's room. My mom asked me if I thought there was a better way I could have handled the celery juice instead of throwing it out, and how I felt about discarding it when my dad had juiced it fresh and brought it up to me. The answer was pretty simple: I knew that not drinking all of the celery juice was the healthiest thing for me, so I did that in the best way I could think of, considering the circumstances. I knew my dad had worked hard to make it every day, but it was better for my body to throw out half of the juice than force myself to drink it all and then feel sick for the rest of the day.

In conclusion, I took responsibility for my well-being, just like I had been taught over the years. After some more talking, my dad decided to only give me half a glass of celery juice. My body felt much better, and eventually the light areas on my skin went away. Soon I was back to full health with the knowledge that I had a gluten allergy and that I shouldn't eat too much of it or it will have effects.

WHAT'S YOUR ENDGAME?

screamed when my 13-year-old daughter landed her axel-toe-loop-jump combination during her ice skating competition. I've seen her fall dozens of times while practicing and leapt for joy as if I'd just received all tens for a performance.

In four short years, she'd gone from skating timidly across the ice to doing axel and double salchow jumps. So, I hadn't really thought about an 'end game' when my friend recounted a conversation she had with another skating mom who insisted that there should be a specific purpose or goal in mind.

Before Mecca began ice skating, my exposure to the sport was limited to what I saw on television—world champions and Olympians. They were strong and graceful—spinning through the air and nailing jumps that seemed impossible.

The reality of ice skating is that millions of kids around the world practice countless hours, endure sprains, fractures, concussions, calluses and bruises, and you will never know their names or see them on television.

Why do they do it? Because they love to skate.

My daughter said, "It's graceful and powerful and you have to be strong and flexible. I like the constant movement. It's fun."

Since we're spending so much time and money on ice skating, shouldn't we have an endgame? Isn't the purpose of playing a sport to get into college, become a professional, or go to the Olympics? Otherwise, *what's the point?* some wonder. Is having fun and socializing enough?

In my opinion, sports are about way more than having fun. They're a core part of our homeschool curriculum. There are life-skills that sports teach that are difficult to find elsewhere. I remember Mecca climbing on walls and rocks and shopping carts when she was younger.

Some frightened mom would warn, "You shouldn't let her do that, she'll fall."

I'd smile pleasantly and say, "Oh, she's okay. Thanks." They didn't know my daughter was a budding gymnast with excellent balance, flexibility and agility.

Once, when I dropped my daughter off for gymnastics camp, her coach stopped in her tracks when she saw us.

"An athlete carries their own gear," she said, pointing at my heavy load. "That's not your mom's responsibility."

Mecca and I looked at each other with surprise. "Oh, we didn't know," I said and promptly handed the gear to my daughter. From that point on, she gladly wielded her heavy backpack with pride.

Even though Mecca loved gymnastics and trained regularly for over six years, she stopped when we moved to Southwest Florida, because she didn't want to find a new gym and wanted to take a break. But the discipline and confidence she gained remains with her to this day.

My daughter tried soccer, karate and running before falling in love with ice skating. She only started to skate because I wanted an indoor activity to keep out of the brutal, humid summer heat. Little did we know her past gymnastics training would give her an advantage of strength and balance, and those skills would transfer perfectly to gliding on two sharp blades over rock-hard ice.

Any sport can provide valuable life skills; my daughter just happens to be an ice skater. Some benefits of ice skating that this proud mama has witnessed are:

- ✔ Self-discipline and self-motivation.

- ✔ Ability to work through physical soreness to achieve her goals. Able to push her body to try new jumps, spins and complicated footwork.

- ✔ Ability to work through frustration when her skating is not going well.

- ✔ Learning to speak up when not getting the instruction she needs in class.

- ✔ Learning to lose graciously.

- ✔ Learning to win graciously.

- ✔ Development of friendships. Ability to support and encourage others.

- ✔ Time management of school work and skating.

One of my proudest moments occurred when Mecca asked to compete at a higher level a few short weeks before a competition, because she felt she had outgrown her current level. She had to convince her coach she was ready to move up, then learn new moves to new music in order to upgrade her program. She worked tirelessly on her routine and gleamed with delight as she performed the routine she wanted, the way she wanted.

Participating in sports as a youth creates a life-long connection to moving the body, which aids in all areas of health, fitness and well-being. The 50- and 60-year-old guys playing pick-up hockey in the arena are the ones who played as kids. My husband competes in 5k runs because he was an athlete growing up, and his synapses are still wired to be physical and active.

Will my daughter be the next Michelle Kwan? Who knows. Will she compete in college or perform with a company like Disney on Ice or on a cruise ship? Maybe. The future will unfold as it will. But my 'endgame' is what's in front of me at this moment: my strong, happy, confident child who's comfortable in her own skin. I think that's more than enough for now.

Should Your Child Have A Goal To Participate In Sports?

Mecca, "Well, I like doing jumps and spins and edges. I like the constant movement. The fact that you have to be strong and graceful...You have to be confident, you have to be brave, you have to be willing to try new things. You have to make sure that you do it right so you don't get hurt and you have to focus."

Link: https://youtu.be/4PvAVrwhqRU

WHAT'S YOUR ENDGAME?

WRITTEN BY MECCA JONES-KELLER

have been figure skating for about five years, and I can't say that I have a set end goal. I don't know if I want to travel the world in skating shows, or become a coach, but I know that I enjoy skating and will continue doing it for as long as I can.

When I started skating, it was just a fun way to get out of the heat, but I soon realized I wanted to get more serious with it as I learned how fun it was to land jumps and spin in different positions. I began in a group Learn to Skate class where I was taught the basic moves and techniques for skating. Eventually, I progressed out of the class and into strictly private lessons with my very own coach, Kandis.

Having a personal coach is necessary when you get to a certain level because as jumps and spins get harder, more instruction and advice is required. Group classes don't provide the individual attention that a personal coach does, but they are great for beginner skaters. I really like having my own coach because she knows my bad habits, skating style, physical limits and personality, so she is able to help me in any way I need. She choreographs my routines to fit my style and always reminds me to smile and show emotion, which is something I struggle with in performing.

Even though I am not the best at expressing emotion on the ice, I still like participating in competitions and shows. I enjoy competing because of the practice and strength it takes to successfully execute multiple rotation jumps, spins and complex footwork with the judges staring at me, watching my every edge, turn and landing. Performing in shows is the same, just without nearly as much pressure. I can relax a little more, but I still have to practice to make sure I put on an entertaining and exciting program for the audience. One of my favorite performances was skating to *Run Run Rudolph* by Kelly Clarkson in our annual Christmas Show. It was a fun routine and I painted my nose red and wore antlers.

Figure skating is a very demanding sport both physically and mentally. It takes physical strength, flexibility and control to improve, but that's only part of it. Corrections are often needed in my skating, since I'm pretty inconsistent when it comes to landing jumps. Unfortunately, my coach isn't always there to point out what I'm doing wrong, so I've learned how to adjust and correct small issues that may arise. This has led me to be more self-aware and conscious of recurring bad habits. I have also learned how to push and challenge myself. There are often jumps, spins and footwork that I don't like doing, or have a hard time with, but they are necessary, so I force myself to do them and practice until I am happy with them. Another big mental aspect of figure skating is nervousness. I get nervous pretty much anytime I'm on the ice, in the spotlight, but I have learned to deal with it. I don't really have any techniques to control my nerves, besides deep breathing, but after skating for years, I know that I just have to go out there and do the best I can, despite how I may feel.

Overall, figure skating is a great sport to challenge the mind and body, and I know it is good for me because it teaches me self-discipline and awareness, as well as forces me to actually smile when I'm on the ice. Even though I don't have any particular goals in mind, I will continue skating because it makes me stronger and I have fun doing it.

Mecca with her long-time coach, Kandis, after a competition.

LINKS TO SANDRA AND THOMAS'S KIDS AND PARENTING VIDEOS:

1. How Does Intuitive Communication Help You Raise Your New Age Kid?
   https://youtu.be/qST7WANT3H0

2. Difference Between Mom vs. Dad Communication
   https://youtu.be/bbu75jBT_wI

3. How Do You Handle Your Child's Disappointment?
   https://youtube/f_qO0EsMM-Y

4. Strong-Willed Children!
   https://youtu.be/zgSTbE0uQKk

5. How to Keep Your Kids Healthy
   https://youtu.be/zmgT5uiDEpY

6. Are You Terrified Your Kids Are Going to Be Like You Were?
   https://youtube/EJJuYO5pm6A

7. The Problem with Being Nice Over Being Honest
   https://youtu.be/flZUC0WNMJM

8. Are You Imposing Your Unfulfilled Desires Onto Your Child?
   https://youtu.be/KjTMDIi5Gig

9. How to Teach Your New Age Kid to Avoid Experiencing a Mean and Cruel World
   https://youtu.be/DWmeI4i4U_0

10. Should Your Child Have a Goal to Participate In Sports?
    https://youtu.be/4PvAVrwhqRU

GLOSSARY:

Affirmations | A declaration that something is true. It is a statement intended to provide encouragement, emotional support, or motivation.

Allopathic | Modern medicine. Uses drugs and/or surgery to fight disease and treat symptoms.

Conscious Being | Awake and aware of one's surroundings, thoughts, and existence.

COVID-19 Global Pandemic | A coronavirus called SARS-CoV-2 caused the COVID-19 disease which spread across several countries and affected tens of millions of people starting around March of 2020. Some symptoms included: fever or chills, cough, shortness of breath or difficulty breathing.

Divine Being/Divine Self | Spirit, True-Self, Authentic-Self, God-Self, as opposed to the personality or ego.

Energy Work | Involves tapping into the body's own frequencies to remove blocks and gather information and direction, ultimately so the body's innate intelligence can heal itself.

Higher Self | The wise, loving, and conscious presence within.

Homeschool | A home education curriculum.

Homeopathic Remedies | Natural remedies that promote the body's own healing process.

Ho'oponopono | A four step ancient Hawaiian forgiveness process taught by Dr. Ihaleakala Hew Len: "I'm Sorry", "Please Forgive Me", "I Love You", "Thank You".

Manifesting | The ability to bring into physical existence through beliefs and attraction.

Master Teacher | One who leads students to uncover their divine nature and develop mastery of Universal Laws.

Metaphysical | Outside of physical reality and the five senses.

Mirroring | Projecting beliefs, fears, judgements and attitudes into the world that are then mirrored back from other people, events and situations.

New Age Kid | Old souls that are wise beyond their years, are connected with and aware of their divine essence, are clear, certain and intuitive. They have been called different names: Indigo Children, Crystal Children, Star Children and Rainbow Children.

Paradigm | Concepts or patterns.

Quantum Field | A place where everything exists—multidimensionality.

Religious Science | Science of Mind was established in 1927 by Ernest Holmes and is a spiritual, philosophical and metaphysical religious movement within the New Thought movement. In general, the term "Science of Mind" applies to the teachings, while the term "Religious Science" applies to the organizations.

Sacro Occipital Technique (SOT) Chiropractor | A unique combination of chiropractic and osteopathy that not only works on aligning one's spine but finds imbalances in the body.

Spiritual Mind Treatments | A form of affirmative prayer practiced by Religious Science Practitioners.

Universal Laws | Laws that govern the Universe. They are impersonal and are always operating. The Universe exists in perfect harmony and order by virtue of these Laws. As written in the Kybalion, the seven Laws are: 1. Mentalism, 2. Correspondence, 3. Vibration, 4. Polarity, 5. Rhythm, 6. Cause and Effect, 7. Gender

RESOURCES TO SUPPORT YOUR JOURNEY:

Additional Reading:

Carolyne Fuqua, Ph.D. | *The Keys to the Kingdom, a New Paradigm for Humanity*

Doreen Virtue | *The Crystal Children*

Helen Schucman and Bill Thetford | *A Course in Miracles*

Joe Vitale and Ihaleakala Hew Len | *Zero Limits: The Secret Hawaiian System for Wealth, Health, Peace, and More*

Lee Carroll and Jan Tober | *The Indigo Children: The New Kids Have Arrived*

Louise Hay | *Heal Your Body: The Mental Causes for Physical Illness and the Metaphysical Way to Overcome Them*

Robie H. Harris and Michael Emberley | *It's So Amazing! A Book about Eggs, Sperm, Birth, Babies, and Families*

Sandra Jones-Keller | *21 Lessons to Empower the New Age Kid*

Sandra Jones-Keller | *Intuitive Communication with Your Baby's Soul*

Thomas Keller | *The MIRROR: Three easy steps to free yourself from fear, anger, and anxiety. And that's just the beginning!*

Three Initiates | *The Kybalion: A Study of the Hermetic Philosophy of Ancient Egypt and Greece*

Books Mentioned In The Essays:

Alyssa Satin Capucilli | *Biscuit*

Cami Berg | *D Is for Dolphin*

Dr. Seuss | *The Tooth Book*

Helen Craig | *Angelina Ballerina*

Karen Beaumont | *I Ain't Gonna Paint No More!*

Karen Beaumont | *I Like Myself!*

Scott Foresman | *Reading: Picture This!*

Watty Piper | *The Little Engine That Could*

Homeschooling Sources:

Carla Hannaford, Ph.D. | *Smart Moves: Why Learning Is Not All in Your Head*

Flash Kids Editors | *Complete Curriculum Workbooks*

Florida Virtual School (FLVS) | The first statewide internet-based public high school in the United States.

Khan Academy | An American non-profit educational organization that creates a set of online tools that help educate students. The organization produces short lessons in the form of videos.

MasterClass | An American online education subscription platform on which students can access tutorials and lectures pre-recorded by experts in various fields.

Outschool | An innovative online education platform that offers a variety of engaging, small-group classes online.

Teachers Pay Teachers | The world's first and largest educational marketplace with 3 million resources. For teachers by teachers.

Various Authors | *Brain Quest Workbooks*

Organizations:

Agape International Spiritual Center, Los Angeles, California

SOTO-USA is a 501(c)(3) non-profit organization which promotes the teaching and research of the Sacro Occipital Technique method of chiropractic.

190

CPSIA information can be obtained
at www.ICGtesting.com
Printed in the USA
LVHW070549171121
703473LV00007B/204